To CLARK

A Gift From your DAD.
Hope it Helps you Figure out
Some of THOSE Tough OLD Bucks.

Hunt Well

Gary Clancy

High Forest, MN

Christmas 2007

HUNTING

Tough Bucks

GARY CLANCY

STOEGER PUBLISHING COMPANY · ACCOKEEK, MARYLAND

Stoeger Publishing
Great Outdoor Books Since 1924

STOEGER PUBLISHING COMPANY
is a division of Benelli U.S.A.

Benelli U.S.A.
Vice President & General Manager:
 Stephen Otway
Vice President of Marketing & Communications:
 Stephen McKelvain

Stoeger Publishing Company
President: Jeffrey Reh
Managing Editor: Harris J. Andrews
Creative Director: Cynthia T. Richardson
Marketing & Communications Manager:
 Alex Bowers
Imaging & Pre-Press Manager: William Graves
National Sales Manager: Jennifer Thomas
Special Accounts Manager: Julie Brownlee
Publishing Assistants: Amy Jones, Amy Sargent

Design & Layout: Peggy Archambault
Proofreader: Amy Jones

Published by Stoeger Publishing Company
17603 Indian Head Highway, Suite 200
Accokeek, Maryland 20607

BK0519
ISBN-10: 0-88317-309-3
ISBN-13: 978-0-88317-309-1
Library of Congress Control Number:
2006921184

Manufactured in the United States of America.

Distributed to the book trade and
to the sporting goods trade by:
Stoeger Industries
17603 Indian Head Highway, Suite 200
Accokeek, Maryland 20607
301-283-6300 Fax: 301-283-6986
www.stoegerpublishing.com

OTHER PUBLICATIONS:

Shooter's Bible
The World's Standard
 Firearms Reference Book
Gun Trader's Guide
Complete Fully Illustrated
 Guide to Modern Firearms
 with Current Market Values

Hunting & Shooting:
The Bowhunter's Guide
Elk Hunter's Bible
High Performance
 Muzzleloading
 Big Game Rifles
High Power Rifle Accuracy:
 Before You Shoot
Hunt Club
 Management Guide
Hunting Whitetails
 East & West
Hunting the Whitetail Rut
Shotgunning for Deer
Taxidermy Guide
Tennessee Whitetails
Trailing the Hunter's Moon
The Turkey Hunter's
 Tool Kit: Shooting Savvy
The Ultimate in Rifle Accuracy
Whitetail Strategies

Firearms:
Antique Guns:
 A Collector's Guide
Gunsmithing Made Easy
How to Buy & Sell Used Guns
Model 1911: Automatic Pistol
Modern Beretta Firearms

Reloading:
The Handloader's Manual of
 Cartridge Conversions 3rd Ed.

Fishing:
Big Bass Zone
Catfishing:
 Beyond the Basics
Fishing Made Easy
Fishing Online:
 1,000 Best Web Sites
Flyfishing for Trout A-Z
Practical Bowfishing

Cooking Game:
The Complete Book of
 Dutch Oven Cooking
Healthy Game & Fish Meals
Wild About Freshwater Fish
Wild About Game Birds
Wild About Seafood
Wild About Venison
Wild About Waterfowl
World's Best Catfish Cookbook

Nature:
The Pocket Disaster
 Survival Guide
The Pocket Survival Guide
U.S. Guide to Venomous
 Snakes and their Mimics

Fiction:
The Hunt
Wounded Moon

Nonfiction:
Escape In Iraq:
 The Thomas Hamill Story

To our grandson Lucas.
You are only two years old as I write these words, but already,
Grandpa can't wait to take you on your first deer hunt.

Contents

INTRODUCTION

In 2004 I wrote a book called *Hunting The Whitetail Rut* for Stoeger Publishing, the same company that is bringing you this book. It's a good book and if you have not read it, put it on your must read list. When I finished that book, my intention was to take a break from writing books for a few years. Books are a lot of work to write and I just did not want to work that hard again for a while. But then *Hunting The Whitetail Rut* started drawing favorable reviews and more importantly to me, was being read and enjoyed by a lot of you. One question I kept getting from those who read *Hunting The Whitetail Rut,* was "what about the rest of the season?" Like me, many of you relish hunting the rut. You plan your vacation to coincide with the rut. You use up your sick days, take time off without pay, skip out of work early and show up late, all to spend a few more hours, a few more days, hunting during the rut. But even with all of the effort we put into hunting that special time of the year, the truth remains that most of us will spend far more days in the deer woods when the rut is not a factor than when it is. In fact, many deer hunters, especially those who hunt with firearms only, have no choice in the matter. Most states do not hold their firearm deer seasons during the rut. And even bowhunters, if they are serious about bowhunting, as most archers are, will clock more hours on stand prior to and after the rut than during the rut. Blackpowder fans who take advantage of special muzzleloader seasons will usually find themselves hunting long after the rut is over, which is when most states slot their special blackpowder hunts. Although a few states have early muzzleloader-only seasons, I am not aware of any states that hold their special muzzleloader hunts during the rut.

So the wheels started turning. An idea for a new book was bubbling in my old brain. One thing I knew from the start was that I didn't want this book to be second best. I did not want to write a book about hunting before and after the rut that left the reader feeling like he was getting leftovers. With all of the humility that I can muster, I believe I have succeeded in that goal with this book, but I'll let you be the final judge of that.

One thing I do know with certainty is that I have written this book as honestly as I know how. There is no "BS" here, no spouting off about things I have not experienced myself and in most cases, experienced for many years. For better or for worse, I do not know any other way to write.

There is a lot of good deer hunting to be enjoyed at times other than the rut. This book is my best effort to help you make those non-rut hunts both enjoyable and more productive.

Gary Clancy
Byron, Minnesota

Chapter One

UNDERSTANDING
the PRE-RUT

Pre-rut is a vague term. What does it mean? Is the pre-rut everything which takes place in the whitetail's world prior to the rut? Or is there a certain signal, a sign which you can use to verify that the pre-rut is in progress? If there really is a difference between early season and the pre-rut, how do you know when one is ending and the other beginning? These are all legitimate questions.

For many hunters, the pre-rut is that two-week to ten-day stretch just prior to when actual breeding begins. It is during this period that bucks are really beginning to "feel their oats," as the old saying goes. There is a lot of rubbing, scraping and general carousing while looking for girls. Very often I have seen this hectic and usually action-filled period referred to in books and magazines as the pre-rut or,

The pre-rut period is when bucks like this begin to travel
more during shooting hours

Many hunters assume that you have to wait for the rut to kick in before you have a good chance at a buck like this one taken by Dennis Williams in southeastern Minnesota. Not true—the pre-rut offers plenty of opportunity for hunting big bucks.

in some cases, advanced or intense pre-rut. I call it the late pre-rut. I've always felt that the pre-rut designation of this period was confusing, but since it has been used for so long, I'm not going to butt heads here. But one thing is certain, the period we call the pre-rut is much longer than the ten-day to two-week stretch that precedes breeding.

I'll agree that the two-week pre-breeding period is, for most serious whitetail hunters, the most important part of the pre-rut. The reason for this is by the time the actual breeding begins, the big breeder bucks are so busy with does that they are seldom seen other than for those brief periods when they must look for another doe in estrous. Prior to the actual start of breeding, however, these bucks are beside themselves with pent up frustration. This is when they are on the prowl nearly non-stop and when they are real suckers for rattling, calling, decoying and scents.

This book is not about hunting during the rut, but it would be impossible to write this book without referring to the rut. That is because everything a buck does from the time he sheds the velvet from his antlers in early September is geared towards the rut. After all, procreation of the species is the sole reason for his existence.

This is how the pre-rut progresses: During the early weeks of bow season, if, as it does in most states, the bow season where you hunt opens in September or very early October, you will find some bucks still hanging out in bachelor groups. They've been together all summer and they are still buddies. They are probably not as close as they were in July, but are still able to tolerate each other's company. But as September wanes, these bucks start to look at their old buddies a little differently. Testosterone is beginning to stir in their loins. Now that old buddy is a competitor.

Generally, these matters are sorted out with just a little posturing and hard stares. The bigger buck lays back his ears, the hair on the back of his neck stands erect and he walks stiff-legged towards the smaller buck. Unless the smaller buck is a real idiot, he gets the drift. True battles are rare during pre-rut. During this period, the pecking order that has actually been in place most of the summer is firmly established. Once ranking is determined within the buck population, it appears to me that subordinate bucks often pay homage to the most dominant buck in the area.

I've seen this many times, but the most dramatic example took place on a September hunt with my old friend Jeff Louderback down in southwest Kansas. Kansas is one of the few states with a September muzzleloader season and I had drawn one of the coveted non-resident muzzleloader tags. One morning I was prowling slowly through the timber along the banks of the nearly dry Cimarron River when I caught a hint of motion up

One of the nice things about hunting the pre-rut period is that the weather is usually as nice as it is going to get during bow season. Not too hot, not too cold.

deadfall, and waited to see what would develop.

The first two bucks were small, but the third one was the caliber of buck for which Kansas is justifiably famous. The big buck began to cross the dry river about 300 yards from where I was positioned, too far for my muzzleloader. So, I just settled in behind the binoculars and watched him. In what would have been the middle of the river, the big buck stopped and that is where he stayed for the next hour.

During that hour nine other bucks crossed the dry riverbed. All nine of them made a point of walking over to the big buck and greeting him. A couple of the smaller bucks, a spike and a forkhorn, actually got the big buck to do a little playful sparring with them. One very nice nine-pointer spent a long time grooming the larger buck's neck and face. A big eight-point and a thirteen-point non-typical that were traveling together walked up to the big boy and each in turn touched their noses to his. The only thing I can figure out is that it was a similar gesture to our shaking hands. It was quite a show and I consider it a privilege to have been there to witness it.

By the way, I never did get to pop a cap

ahead. I froze in my tracks and watched as a doe and fawn made their way across the dry riverbed. I had to wait until they were out of sight before I could continue on my way, but before the doe and fawn were gone, two more deer arrived on the scene. Then two more and another and another. I had stumbled onto a whitetail convention. I hunkered down behind a

Subtle signs, like deer hair on a barbed wire fence indicating where deer are crossing, are what the pre-rut hunter is looking for.

Younger bucks, like this one, react to the rut later than mature bucks, so your best bet for a young buck is to hunt the food sources.

on that monster Kansas buck, but I did take that thirteen-point non-typical. It was a very nice consolation prize!

By the middle of September, the more dominant bucks are beginning to do quite a bit of rubbing. This will escalate with each passing week. The younger bucks, other than to help remove the velvet from their antlers, are not into the rubbing thing as yet. They will get started later in October. This is why I always get excited when I find a number of rubs in an area in September. I know that there is a very good chance that those rubs were made by a better-than-average buck.

In fact, as I write these words it is September 27, 2004. On the 24th, while doing a little snooping after a morning on stand, I found a half dozen rubs on aspen trees, each sapling about as big around as a can of beans. A little more detective work and I found two scrapes. Neither was of the caliber you will find in late October and early November, but they were scrapes by golly and in my experience, little bucks do not scrape this early in the year. I was pumped. I moved a stand and was waiting there that evening. Three does and fawns

came first, followed by two more. All five fed out into the standing soybeans.

Just at sunset a pair of six-point bucks emerged from the thick timber and began to feed. I had seen the pair of six-pointers that morning and I was certain they were not responsible for the rubs or scrapes. And then, right at the end of legal shooting time, Mr. Big made his grand entry. A good mature ten-pointer. Unfortunately, he saw the pair of six-pointers out in the field and walked right out to join them, passing by too far for me to shoot. But I know where he is hanging out, so there is

Scouting for rubs and rub lines during an early season hunt can reveal where bucks are beginning to congregate.

There are a few regions where some of the bucks may not yet have shed their velvet during the early part of bow season.

a fair chance I will get a chance at him yet this fall. Without those early season rubs, I would probably not have seen that buck because I would have been set up in one of my other stands which would not have allowed me to see that soybean field.

By the second week of October, most bucks are traveling alone. However, as with everything else when it comes to whitetail deer, there are always exceptions. Even during the rut, when bucks do not normally tolerate each other at all, I have on rare occasions seen a pair of bucks traveling together. It may have been that the two were on the trail of the same hot doe when I saw them, or maybe one had just whipped the other and was ushering the loser out of the area. I know that in the world of the whitetail, always and never are two words that I do not employ. So I would not say that bucks never travel

together as October gets long in the tooth, but it is rare.

Mature bucks continue to make more rubs and pick up the pace on scrape production. Smaller bucks start to get in on the rubbing and scraping action. There is still very little mid-day activity, but early morning movement lasts a little longer now and business picks up in the evening a tad earlier as well.

At night, the bigger bucks spend a lot of time feeding and laying on that layer of fat that will sustain them through the rigors of the rut, but they also begin to do more traveling as they check out the doe groups in the area. Don't want to miss that odd early estrous doe you know.

Scraping action goes into high gear during that last week of October in most areas of the country. I've always thought that this period belongs to the rut and not the pre-rut, but the problem with me making that change here is that it would be confusing to many readers who have grown up with scraping and pre-rut being nearly synonymous. So, let's leave this intense scraping period in the pre-rut for now.

This will last right up until the bucks become so charged up and ready to breed that they spend most of their time chasing not-quite-ready does all over the woods. When you see this happening, you know that the chase phase of the rut is in progress and that actual breeding is just a few days away.

Most serious rubbing, like this stripped sapling, is done at night.

Chapter Two

A GAME PLAN *for* EARLY SEASON WHITETAIL

A friend of mine stopped by one evening, mid-way through the first week of archery deer season. I had just pulled into the garage after an evening hunt and since Sean was still dressed in camouflage, I assumed he had been out that evening as well. Usually when one of my buddies shows up at that time of the evening, they either need help dragging one out, or help tracking.

"What's it going to be," I asked by way of a greeting, "a drag rope or my lantern?"

"Neither," was Sean's sullen reply. "Looks like I'm done until the rut kicks in. I had a few does and one pretty decent buck coming to that alfalfa field up on top of the ridge the first two evenings, but I haven't seen them now for three evenings in a row. I guess they moved somewhere else.

Some states like Kansas, where this magnificent whitetail buck was taken,
have early season muzzleloader hunts.

Early in the season, when the weather is warm and you know that you are going to be perspiring when hunting, odor control becomes imperative to success.

That's the way it is early in the season you know. If you don't get them that first day or two you can forget it. "Oh well, I've got a week's vacation the first week of November. I'll get after them hard then."

Most of the bowhunters I know feel pretty much like Sean when it comes to the early season. That's because the only game plan most bowhunters have for the early season is the obvious one, namely to hunt the deer coming to fields or, in some big woods situations, to clear-cuts. Hey, it's a good plan too, for as long as it lasts, but in most cases it is not going to last long. Deer, especially mature bucks and does, are quick to pick up on the fact that they are being hunted. Once that happens you can forget about taking a mature deer on a field or clear-cut. At this point you have a couple of choices: You can hang up your

When hunting field edges early in the season, be sure to have several early season field edge stands so that you do not quickly alert the deer to the fact that they are being hunted.

bow for a month or so and wait for the rut to kick in, or you can put together a game plan which will allow you to squeeze a lot more action out of those early weeks of the season. Here is the game plan I use. You are welcome to copy it, modify it to fit your own style or ignore it and stay home and clean the garage while I go hunting. The choice is yours.

GETTING THE MOST OUT OF A FIELD

All summer deer filter out into fields and clear-cuts in the evening to feed. When the bow season opens, hunters are waiting in stands on the edge of the field or clear-cut to take advantage of the situation. If you connect on that first evening, there is no problem, but if you do not, you now have to figure out how to get down out of that tree stand without alerting every deer in the field to your presence. If you spook the deer, the next evening there will be fewer deer in the field during shooting light, if you spook them again the next evening, by the third evening the field will probably still be vacant when darkness settles in. The keys to getting the most out of your early season fields or clear-cuts are these: (1) have more than one stand on a field so that you will not be inclined to hunt a stand when the wind is wrong, (2) try to have more than one field to hunt, (3) be sure that you can get into your stand without alerting deer that will later be using the field (if you cannot, forget that stand site), (4) consider using a ground blind instead of a tree stand (a ground blind, either a commercial pop-up type blind like my favorite, the Double Bull, or a blind crafted from native materials is often easier to slip into and vacate without being detected. If you are going to use a ground blind it should be in place well before the season so that deer become accustomed to its presence), (5) if you can arrange it, have someone drive into the field—with the landowner's permission of course—and pick you up at or near your stand (when the vehicle arrives the deer will temporarily scatter out of the field, giving you time to climb down from your stand and get back to the vehicle without having alerted deer to your presence—I've hunted the same field for over a week just by employing this tactic), (6) never hunt a field or clear-cut in the morning. The only thing you will accomplish is to ruin your chances for the evening.

WHEN THE ACTION ON THE FIELD DRIES UP—THEN WHAT?

Eventually however, no matter how careful you are, deer are going to catch on and the evening action in the field will dry up. Deer don't just quit feeding in the field. Instead they adjust their feeding schedule, which simply means that they do not enter the field until after shooting hours have expired. But the neat thing is that they still tend to get up out of their beds at the same time each day. Now, however, instead of trucking right straight to that favorite field or clear-cut, they tend to mosey along, browsing here and there, taking their sweet old time and then hanging back from the field just killing time waiting for darkness. Some guys call them staging areas, others call them transition zones. Whatever you call them, these are the places to hang your stand when the action on the field ceases. Most of the time this staging will take place 50 to 100 yards away from the edge of the field, but if the edge cover is heavy, bucks will sometimes stage much closer. Trails, tracks, droppings and rubs are your best signs.

SPEAKING OF RUBS

I am amazed at how many bowhunters still lump rubs, scrapes and the rut all into one neat little package. The truth is that rubs are the best early season buck sign you can find. The rubs you find early are rubs made by the dominant buck in the area. Little bucks don't start doing their thing until later in the fall. That's why I spend a lot of time looking for and following rub lines during the early weeks of the season. Find a good rub line and you

Because some plants may still be growing during early season hunts, you may find it necesssary to re-trim some shooting lanes that you established while hanging your stands a week or two earlier.

have found the number one location in all of the woods for a crack at Mr. Big.

AND THEN THERE ARE THE ACORNS

Most of us tend to assume that when deer vacate fields that it is because of hunting pressure. Often it is, but just as often you can blame acorns. Whitetail deer are bonkers over acorns. Frequently the early weeks of the season will coincide with the time when acorns are dropping. When this happens, deer are often so busy scarfing up acorns in the woods that they don't get out to the fields until well after dark.

I've got a little spot over in western Wisconsin that I hunt that is a perfect example. It's a flat area, probably ten acres in size, studded with giant white oaks. Deer bed on the high ridge above the little flat and make their way across the flat in late

Spying on deer feeding in a field from a long distance will allow you to pinpoint where the deer are exiting and entering the field.

afternoon on their way to feed in the soybean, alfalfa and corn fields down below. I've got a couple of stands hung on the flat to intercept them as they move through. But when the acorns start dropping big time, which is usually mid-September to early October in this neck of the woods, the deer don't just move through, they congregate on that little flat to munch acorns. If I did not know about that little flat and the acorn connection, I would still be sitting on one of my stands along the edges of one of those fields wondering what happened to all of the deer.

By the way, the best way to prepare for the acorn drop is to know in advance which trees are loaded with mast. I visit my hunting areas in late summer armed with a pair of good binoculars and search the tops of the oaks for clusters of acorns. When I find a tree, or better yet, a group of oaks loaded with acorns, I will often hang my stand then or prepare a stand site and clear shooting lanes so that when I come back to hunt all I have to do is pop a stand up and I'm in business.

DEER LIKE TO DRINK TOO

For many years, like most of the deer hunters I know, I never gave much thought to where deer drink. But the last few years I've been paying a lot of attention to this

Early season hunting can mean very warm temperatures, so be sure to drink plenty of water to avoid dehydration.

matter and it has paid big dividends. Early in the season, the weather is often very warm and deer need to drink. Usually they will tank up in the morning before bedding down for the day and will then drink again in late afternoon when they get up. If it is very warm, they will sometimes slip away for a drink at mid-day.

The best situations for hunting near water occur where water sources are scarce. This situation concentrates deer at the available water source and this can lead to lots of action. The other side of that coin is that in many prime whitetail habitats there is so much water available that hunting over water would appear to be a waste of time. I say appear-to-be, because I have noticed over the years that even when water is readily available at a number of different locations, deer, like some people, have favorite watering holes. In the case of whitetail deer, the key is seclusion. Deer may drink from that clear, cool stream trickling through the pasture at night, but you won't catch them drinking there during shooting hours. Instead they will take their drink from that scummy, stagnant pond back in the woods, the one almost choked by briars and vines. Find a secluded pond or spring seep back in good whitetail habitat and I'll bet you will find the soft earth along it's edges littered with deer tracks.

That's my early season game plan. Field edges first, then the transition areas, rublines, the acorn drop and watering holes. We will cover all of them in more detail, but I wanted to give you an overview of how the early season stacks up. If I stick to my early season game plan, I can almost guarantee, that by the time my buddy Sean takes that week's vacation to hunt the rut in November, I will have already tagged a nice buck and a bonus doe or two.

SO YOU WANT A VELVET BUCK?

There are a couple dozen shoulder-mounts of nice whitetail bucks hanging in our home. Know which one gets the most attention from visitors? If you guessed the one with the biggest rack, you guessed wrong. The buck that draws the most attention from hunters and non-hunters alike is a full velvet buck that I took while bowhunting in Montana a few years ago. His rack is not all that big, but with those soft, fuzzy antlers and that slick, short-haired summer coat, I've got to admit he is a strikingly beautiful animal.

Some hunters could care less about taking a buck in velvet, but for others it's a quest. If you fit into the latter category, your best odds of accomplishing that feat is to plan an early September hunt. Your best bets right now are to hunt in North Dakota, Montana, Wyoming or across the border in Manitoba. All of these states and the Canadian province have archery seasons which open in either early September or late August.

Many other states, such as Minnesota and Wisconsin, open the archery season in mid-September. There will still be a few bucks in velvet then, but most will have shed their velvet. When I hunt specifically for a buck in velvet, I always figure that the last week of August and the first week of September will provide me with the best opportunities. By the second week of September many of the bucks will have shed their velvet.

I've noticed that if the summer has been unseasonably cool, as it was this summer, that the bucks will shed their velvet earlier than normal. I was doing some scouting in late August (the 29th

Heading out for the evening stand.

to be precise), and spent the evening sitting up on a hill with binoculars and spotting scope, spying on deer which were feeding in an alfalfa field. Eleven different bucks came to that field that evening. Nine of the eleven were already clean. Only the two biggest bucks, both mature deer of 3 years or older were still in velvet. I don't know why a cool summer has this affect on when the bucks shed velvet, but I've seen it several times over the years.

Chapter Three

FOOD RULES

Sure I get a big thrill out of finding a string of hot scrapes and hunting over them. Ditto for rubs. And I have killed some good bucks by hunting what I call "chase sign,"—the running tracks left behind by a buck or more commonly two or more bucks engaged in the ancient ritual of the rut. I would not ignore any of these signals of whitetail activity and I would not suggest that you do either. But sometimes I think we get so wrapped up in hunting areas with this exciting sign, that we overlook the obvious. A field of corn or soybeans is just not exciting. My heart has never raced at the mere sight of a green field. No, hunting food sources or the trails leading to them does not normally make the heart race and the adrenalin pump. Nevertheless, when the rut is not a factor, this is the most consistent tactic you have in the game plan for putting a buck on the ground.

Late in the year it is tough to beat standing corn
as a whitetail food source.

Scout cameras are a great way to stay informed on what deer are currently feeding on in the area you are hunting.

are not. They are blue-collar hunters. They hail from all parts of our country and have different hunting styles. These men and women have their favorite tricks and tactics just like you and I. But one thing that they all have in common is that they never overlook the primary food sources.

Deer activity at the food source is more predictable than deer activity along rub lines or strings of scrapes. That is because whitetail deer are eating machines, consuming an average of eight pounds of food each day. While it is true that they do a lot of this munching at night, they are also big on the evening meal and breakfast. And, like us, they will usually have a little something around mid-day as well.

Very few whitetail deer are shot while lying in their beds. To be vulnerable, a whitetail has to be up and moving. A buck or doe spends more time on its hooves either eating or traveling to and from the chow line than it does for any other reason. That alone is reason enough to make hunting food sources, or the trails that lead to them, a first rate tactic.

Before we go any further in this discussion, let me dispel a rumor that has been spread around whitetail camps for as long as I can remember: When the rut is in gear, bucks are so focused on sex that they

That's a bold statement to make I suppose, but I stand by my words.

It has been my good fortune to spend more hours, more days and more months each year in the pursuit of whitetail deer than most hunters are able to tally in a decade. I'm grateful for that opportunity. Sure I've spent many enjoyable days hunting over scrapes, or rubs, or the hottest chase sign I could find, and I plan to continue doing so during the seasons to come. But I have seen more deer and killed more deer on or near food sources than I have on any of those other more dramatic locations. And this is not just my experience. It has been my pleasure to get to know and hunt with some of the most knowledgeable whitetail hunters in this nation. Some are famous in hunting circles, with names and faces you would recognize, but most forget all about eating. That simply is not true. I've killed a fair number of bucks during the rut and I've yet to shoot any that had an empty paunch. It is true that bucks become less and less interested in food as the rut progresses and rarely take time to eat enough to make up for the energy they expend while seeking, chasing and tending does. This is why a big buck will often lose around 20 percent of its body weight during the course of the rut. It also explains why a buck that might be carrying an inch of white fat on it's rump and a half-inch or better layered across its back in mid-October will not have a trace of fat left on its body by the time the rut winds down. Bucks might not eat much during the rut, but they do eat.

Of course being convinced that food source areas are worth hunting is the easy part. The real work starts when you must try to identify the food source. In some cases this is actually very easy to do, but other times, it can take a lot of detective work. It all depends upon the options available to the deer. Let me give you a real life example of what I mean by that.

One January, I made a trip to Alabama to hunt with Bill Fargasson, the guy who builds the ScentTite blind. And yes, if you are curious, the blind really does work as advertised. But that is not my main point for mentioning this

When food is plentiful, as in the early archery season, deer feed on such a wide variety of foods that it is often impossible to narrow the list of favorites down to just one or two.

Sometimes it pays to take an evening off from the hunt to do some long range scouting to locate where the deer are feeding. Once you've got that information, you can move in and set up a stand to take advantage of the movement to the food source.

There should be some serious rubs showing up about the same time as those big scrapes. If they are not serious, you are probably not dealing with a big buck.

particular hunt. By late January in central Alabama, the deer, turkeys, squirrels and other critters have cleaned up the majority of the acorns in the hardwood bottoms. Wild grasses and leafy foliage have succumbed to a combination of the end of the natural growing season and a series of hard freezes. If not for the food plots, which in the case of Bill's farm were green fields planted to rye grass and other legumes, the deer would be hard pressed to find a respectable meal. Bill had about a dozen small food plots on his farm and the deer were hammering them. It was simply a matter of picking the right field. On the third evening I did and I shot the seventh buck that entered the field that evening: a handsome, high-racked eight-pointer. With the deer concentrated on the limited food sources available to them, it would have been silly to hunt for them anywhere else. When food sources are at a premium, as they were on that January hunt in Alabama, deer have limited options and that really works in favor of us hunters.

Of course, sometimes the opposite is true. Whitetail deer have what biologists refer to as "catholic taste," which does not mean that the Pope rules in the whitetail world, but that the whitetail deer will eat darn near anything. That is why the more food sources available, the more difficult it is to pinpoint a specific food source to hunt over. Take early October in the Midwest, where I live, for example. If the mast crop has been good, the woods

are full of fallen acorns. Grasses and leafy plants are still abundant. Apples are dropping nightly. The last of the soybeans are being harvested and corn is being picked at a rapid pace so it's easy pickings for leftover grain. For a little variety the alfalfa and clover are both still lush. Trying to select the one food source that the deer find most appealing out of a smorgasbord like that is nearly impossible. The reason it is so difficult is that deer, when given the opportunity, much prefer to nibble on a little of this and a little of that until they have sampled it all, rather than filling their tanks on, let's say, a diet of straight corn.

There are no easy answers for this problem. When deer are not concentrated on a specific food source, often the best you can do is pick the food source that you think the deer are keying on the most, or as I often do, choose the food source nearest where you think the deer are bedding. At least that way, you have the best chance of intercepting the deer in early evening as they rise and begin to feed or perhaps catch them grabbing a snack before turning in for the morning.

Anytime food is in abundance, pinpointing a specific food source to hunt over is difficult and quite frankly is often impossible because as I mentioned earlier, whitetail deer are wonderful opportunists when it comes to diet. But when the choices dwindle, as they always do, it becomes easier and easier to narrow down the whitetail's dining options. This is when food rules.

Chapter Four

WHITETAILS
& WATER

Proving once again that we are never too old to learn, I have, in recent years, begun paying attention to water sources when it comes to hunting whitetail deer. As with many things in life, I wish I had started paying attention to water sources earlier because they are excellent locations for stand sites. In fact, at certain times during the season, hunting near the places where whitetail drink is so good that if I were fortunate enough to own my own hunting land, the first thing I would do is dig a pond or two in secluded locations where the deer would feel comfortable grabbing a quick drink.

Under normal conditions a whitetail will drink two and sometimes three times during a 24-hour period: usually when they get up from their beds in the afternoon, before they bed down for the morning and often once at mid-day (if the water source is close enough to their bedding area and secluded enough that they feel comfortable drinking

Deer need three things to survive: food, cover, and water. Many hunters key on food and cover, but forget about water, making a big mistake.

Early in the season when the weather is warm, deer will drink twice and sometimes three times during a 24-hour period.

there at mid-day). If the weather is on the hot side, just like you and I, they will drink more often. Ditto for when the rut is on. Even if the weather is cool, bucks must drink a lot of water just to stay on their feet during this hectic time. When the bucks are chasing does hard, they must drink or die of dehydration. If warm weather lasts through the rut, the bucks must drink even more often. Does also, after being chased all over creation by the amorous bucks, work up a real thirst. When the doe comes to get a drink, guess who follows her to the watering hole? Often this heavy drinking really gets started during late pre-rut.

A few years ago, I was sitting in a stand that overlooked a little seep. It wasn't much of a seep, not much bigger than a laundry basket, but it was the preferred drinking location for deer in that neck of the woods. Pre-rut action was hot and heavy. As I nearly always do when this is the case, I stayed in that stand all day. In fact, because I was seeing so many deer, I hunted that stand for three days in a row, sitting from dark-to-dark each day. I lost count of how many deer, bucks and does, stopped for a drink at that seep, but one buck with a messed up, easy to distinguish seven-point rack visited the seep six times in one day. That three day sit represents the most action I have ever personally witnessed when hunting over water, but many times I have seen three or four bucks come to drink in a day. Those are pretty good stats in my book.

Whitetail deer are very opportunistic critters, so they will drink wherever water is available to them. However, they are also very shy creatures and if the water source is a creek, river, lake or pond where they must expose themselves, they will typically utilize these water sources only under cover of darkness. You will find plenty of tracks in the mud along the bank at these places, but do not be misled by the tracks. Tracks made at night do not do you much good. That is why I look for places where the cover-loving whitetail will feel comfortable drinking during the day. A small pond situated deep in the woods, a spring seep, maybe a muddy little creek trickling through a nasty tangle of brush and bramble—these are the kind of places where a whitetail prefers to drink.

When my friend Tom Indrebo, who with his wife Laurie, runs Bluff Country Outfitters near Alma, Wisconsin, decided to put a few ponds on his land, it would have been much easier and less expensive to simply bulldoze the ponds at the bottom of draws. But Tom knows as much about whitetail deer as anyone I have ever met and he knew that if he placed his ponds at the bottom of the draws that the deer would utilize them mostly at night. So instead, Tom spent the extra money and took the extra time to dig his ponds high on the ridges near the thickets where he knew the deer preferred to bed. This location not only made it convenient for deer to grab a drink late in the afternoon when rising from their beds, and again

Deer are especially fond of drinking at small, isolated seeps near or in heavy cover.

in the morning before turning in for the day, but because the ponds are in cover, deer feel comfortable visiting them at any hour of the day. Tom's guests have taken some mighty fine bucks from stands and ground blinds situated near those ponds. It is interesting, but not surprising, that many of those bucks have fallen during the middle of the day.

One mistake it is easy to make when scouting for potential watering sites is to assume that like us humans, deer would prefer to drink from a clear, cold, flowing stream instead of a stagnant, warm, scummy pond. But deer do not think like we do. If the choice is between sucking warm, muddy water from a secluded pond tucked deep in heavy cover or exposing themselves to drink

*The best watering sites
are near prime bedding areas.
Deer will go a long way to feed,
but not to drink.*

*Sometimes you get lucky
and can use the water source as a scent
free entrance and exit to your stand.*

from the clear flowing stream, the deer will do their daytime drinking at the pond.

Late in the season, when it is cooler and when snow covers the ground in many parts of the country, it is easy to assume that deer do not need to drink or that they get what fluids they need by eating snow, which is simply not true. It has been my experience that while deer will eat snow, they prefer to drink water. I've watched them use their front hooves to break through thin ice to create a hole from which to drink. Find a spring or a seep that does not freeze up in all but the most severe cold and odds are excellent that you will have found a great stand location for late season muzzleloader and archery hunts.

No matter what time of the year I hunt over water, I have noticed that deer are often very nervous when approaching a pond to drink. This is true even when they have not been hunted near the pond before. My guess is that this extra caution near drinking sites is a trait passed down from generation to generation of deer and is a direct result of deer being preyed on for thousands of years at watering holes. After all, it did not take the big predators nearly as long to catch onto the fact that a pond is a great place to grab a venison dinner as it did this old whitetail hunter.

Chapter Five

The MOST IMPORTANT RUBS

I was hunting a friend's farm down in northwest Missouri in early October and the weather had been unseasonably hot. Of all of the weather conditions Mother Nature can dish up, I hate hot weather the worst. In my experience deer just do not move worth a hoot in hot weather. But I was there, so I hunted. To make matters worse, I had not been able to find much buck sign. The best stand site I had was situated at the junction of two long ditches, which might be called gullies or draws in other parts of the country. There were a smattering of rubs along both of the ditches (not really enough to call it a rub line), but those rubs were the best buck sign I had been able to find after extensive scouting, so I decided to concentrate my morning hunts at the junction of those two ditches. On the third morning of

If you are a deer hunter, your heart rate goes up a notch when you find a rub like this one.

You can be sure that rubs like these were made by a buck wearing impressive headgear. Smaller bucks may come and work over a large rub that has been started by a larger buck, but smaller bucks do not initiate rubs of this caliber.

my hunt, I was in my stand before first light and already it was warm and muggy. I had not seen a single buck during the first two days of hunting and had seen only one doe and fawn. Let's just say that my optimism was waning. Then I saw the top of a little cedar tree waving in the wind. Except that there was no wind. Even with binoculars I could not find the buck I hoped was making that cedar tree shake, but I figured it had to be a buck. With each minute it grew lighter and the cedar tree kept on shaking. Finally, I caught a glimpse of hide through the branches of the tree and then the buck, finally satisfied with the mark he had left on the trunk of the cedar tree, came walking down the trail in my direction. It was an easy shot. I've been hunting whitetail deer for a long time and have been lucky enough to have spent more time in the places the whitetail calls home than most. You would think then, that the sight of a sapling with the bark rubbed off of it

Following rub lines is one of the best ways of figuring out an individual buck's travel pattern.

would be old hat by now. But I am happy to report that such is not the case. Buck rubs still trip my trigger and I'll tell you why. Some hunters claim that a buck rub only means that a buck was once at that spot and that it has no bearing on where that buck might be today or tomorrow. That is true if you find that rub on say the first of November. When the breeding period of the rut draws near, bucks make rubs at random. In good deer country, rubs show up everywhere, seemingly overnight. Many of these rubs are made when bucks find themselves in the presence of does. Basically, they are showing off for the girls. All of you guys will understand. That is why you find so many rubs along the edges of fields. The does are out there eating and the young bucks are beating up trees hoping to get their attention. It doesn't work, but they never seem to give up. Some of the rubs you find in late October and early November were made when two bucks met. They flex their muscles for each other, each trying to convince the other that he is too big and too bad to take on. Destroying a sapling is one way of flexing their muscles. And some rubs are simply a buck's way of blowing off steam as the testosterone builds in his system. Sure these rubs all act as communicators in the whitetail's world, but betting that a buck will return to visit one of these rubs, or even walk the same trail again, is a long shot at best.

But find that rub in September or even early October and by golly you will have my interest. Find some more rubs to go with it, what is commonly called a "rub line" and now you are talking some serious information, information you can use to get the drop on a big buck. There are two reasons why a rub line discovered before mid-October gets my juices flowing. One, is the fact that the biggest bucks make the earliest rubs. When I find a good rub line between mid-September and the first part of October I can be reasonably sure that it was made by a mature buck. I like to hunt mature bucks. By late October and early November every buck in the woods is making rubs. When all the bucks are rubbing, it is impossible to use rub lines to key in on a particular deer.

The second reason why my heart rate goes up a notch or two when I find a good string of rubs during the early part of the bow season is that I know that I can use those rubs to help me formulate a game plan for getting a shot at the buck that made the rubs. Sometimes I hang a stand overlooking the rub line itself and wait for the buck to make a return trip. No, the buck is not coming back to check the rubs. In fact, only rarely does a buck actually take the time to even sniff his handiwork, but very often that string of rubs will be located along the trail the buck is using to move from his bedding area to the food source or back again. There are worse places to sit. Sometimes, if I can follow it far enough, a rub line will take me

Rub lines are often easier to identify if you get down on your knees and look at the terrain from the eye level of a buck.

to even better places for a stand (a funnel perhaps, a fence crossing or better yet an open gate the deer are walking through). Most of the time I can follow a rub line to the buck's bedding area. That's really some valuable hunting information.

I don't often hunt in a bedding area, but I like to haunt the fringes of it, especially during morning hunts. The neat thing about locating a bedding area is that even if I don't get a crack at that buck early in the season, odds are he will use that bedding area off and on all season long. These early season rubs are not easy to find. There are not many of them because sadly there are not many mature bucks to make them. In fact, in some areas, where a 2½ year-old buck is the bull of the woods, you won't find any early rubs. The only way I know to locate early rubs is to start walking.

When you find a lone rub, look in all directions for the next. Sometimes it helps to squat down on your heels and look from a deer's perspective. I use binoculars a lot when scouting out rub lines. It is

surprising how well a rub shows up with binoculars that I did not even see with the naked eye. If you can't find more than just a rub or two, don't give up on the place, maybe the buck has not finished his handiwork yet. A buck might take a week or more to produce a rub line. Check back in a few days and see if you can find anymore rubs.

Taking my own advice paid off big time for me during an early October hunt in western Illinois. As soon as I arrived I headed directly to an area where I had found a super rub line the previous October. I was confident that I had seen the buck which had made that rub line, and the landowner assured me that he had seen that same buck several times after the season was over, so I was reasonably sure that the buck had made it through the hunting season.

I guess I was expecting too much, but when I got to the area that had been "rub city" the previous season, all I could find were two fresh rubs on the cedar trees that dominated the ridge. Disappointed, I went looking elsewhere and hunted a different part of the farm for a couple of days. But I did not forget about that cedar ridge. When I returned on the third day after my initial visit, it was evident that a buck had been busy *since* my initial visit.

There were now eight rubs staggered

Cedar trees, such as this one, are one of a whitetail's favorite species to rub.

Look closely and you can see the healed over scars from previous years of rubbing. The same buck? Maybe, maybe not. But one thing is certain, the buck that did this is a brute.

*Early in the season, rubs are the best
buck signs you can find.*

along that ridge. The buck, or at least a buck, was traveling the ridge repeatedly and adding a rub or two on each trip. I already had a stand in position from the previous season, so the next morning, I was in it just before first light. When the nine-point buck came ghosting through those cedar trees in the faint light of the new day, I knew in an instant that it was not the monster I had seen the previous season, but I also knew that he was way too good for me to pass up. In my experience, if it is a mature buck you have your sights set on, then rubs are the best early season sign you can find. Even if you do not actually hunt right on the rub line, you can use the rub line to help determine a buck's route of travel and to help pinpoint food sources and bedding areas. That is valuable information that is hard to come by if you don't pay attention to rub lines early in the season.

Get low and use binoculars to search ahead for the next rub in the line.

Chapter Six

WHAT OCTOBER LULL?

I am real tired of listening to bowhunters complain about the so-called "October Lull." This whole business about the so-called "October Lull" has been blown way out of proportion. To listen to hunters whine about the hunting in early to mid-October, you would think all of the deer migrated out of the country or crawled into burrows. It's not really those grown up hunters I'm concerned about though. If they want to stay home and clean the garage and wash windows on those October weekends when they could be hunting, that is their business. What makes me sad is that a lot of young or inexperienced bowhunters do not even bother to hunt until late October just because they have heard and read so much about how tough it is earlier in the month. These hunters are

Scott Anderson is all smiles as he poses with a dandy October Lull 10-pointer.

Use binoculars to find the oaks that hold the greatest mast crop and then hunt near them during the October Lull when those acorns are hitting the ground.

pink light of dawn and in the last glow of dusk, if they show at all. But by golly it is still hunting and looking back over the years, I can recall a lot of good hunts I've enjoyed when all of the experts said I should be going fishing or sneaking in a last round of golf. I remember one such mid-October hunt in the midwest where I do a lot of my hunting, I was enjoying what we call Indian Summer. The days were warm and sun-drenched, the nights just right for sleeping with the window open in the bedroom. It was nice enough that I gave some thought to going walleye fishing that morning. But I didn't, and I'm sure glad.

It was too warm for frost, but a veil of dew made it easy to sneak quietly into my stand. I was all settled in my stand a few minutes before shooting light. I've always liked that time of the morning when the new day is just breaking. The night critters are scurrying for the bedroom and the day critters and all of the birds start thinking about having some breakfast. In fact, I was watching a nuthatch walk upside down on the trunk of a pock-marked box elder tree when I heard a rustle in the damp leaves that did not sound like a squirrel. When you hunt a lot, squirrels sound like squir-

missing out on some good hunting and some of the most pleasant weather of the season. No, I'm not into sugar-coating, so I won't begin to pretend that early and mid-October is my favorite time to bowhunt.

Sure it's tough. But then I figure, if I wanted it easy, I would never have picked up the bow in the first place. Deer don't move as much now as they will in a few weeks. You won't see numbers of deer, and the bigger bucks will likely only show at rels, and everything else is suspect. I listened hard and heard the rustling again. It was coming from my left, an area that had been logged off a few years prior. The logger had left all of the tree tops where they fell and now they were grown through with briar and bramble. My farmer friend who let me hunt the place called it "a hell of a mess." The truth is deer like to bed in places like that. The rustling came again. I put the binoculars to my face and picked apart the cover. Could be a racoon, or maybe a possum. But something told me it was a deer. Then I caught a flash of gray too high up to belong to a coon or possum. A doe slipped quickly through a gap in the tangle of briars. A buck drifted through right behind her. Moments later, when the doe led the buck out onto the little flat on which I was perched, I could tell he was interested in the doe. The old gal would stop to chomp an acorn and the buck would stick his nose on her rump. He wasn't interested in any acorn.

The two deer were about 75 yards from my stand. If the buck had been alone, I would have grunted to him, but I knew that he would not leave the doe to investigate a grunt or doe bleat, so I just sat tight clenching the grip of the familiar Mathews in my left fist and waited to see what would develop. The doe ambled

Many experienced bowhunters, like Myles Keller, spend more time scouting with binoculars and spotting scopes during the October Lull than they do actually sitting in treestands.

about for a few minutes feeding on acorns, the nine-point buck never more than a step or two behind. Twice I heard the buck grunt and I thought he might press the issue, but he did not. When the doe started up the ridge I figured my chances of getting a shot at the buck were going with her. But then a second buck, a pretty fair eight-pointer, showed up on the scene. You could tell by the way he acted that he had caught a whiff of something he liked drifting on the morning breeze.

The eight-pointer was not as patient as the other buck. He made a quick dash at the doe with his neck stretched out and his head low to the ground like they do. The doe did not much care for the buck's advances. She scooted away from the buck and hustled back for the heavier cover the treetops provided. Her route took her seventeen steps from the base of the basswood in which I perched. Both bucks were right on her tail. I came to full draw and grunted with my voice. Both bucks skidded to a halt. I dropped the string and watched the fletching disappear right where it was supposed to. That's a real good feeling for a bowhunter.

I could not see the buck go down, but after a short dash into the treetops, I heard him crash. That's when my right leg started to jump. It always does when it is over. That buck, which fell on October 13th, was no fluke. My journals indicate that I have taken nearly two dozen whitetail deer, including several nice bucks, during the first three weeks of October. No, early to mid-October is not my favorite time to bowhunt whitetail deer. Like you, I prefer November. But over the years, I have learned that there are a number of ways to cash in on early and mid-October hunts. Many of these we will cover in detail in this book. But here is an overview of the tactics I use to make the "October Lull" anything but dull.

THE OCTOBER MINI-RUT

You won't find the October mini-rut discussed in scientific journals, but that does not mean it doesn't happen. For years I have witnessed a spurt of rutting activity in mid-October. Specifically between October 11th and the 15th. I kept my mouth shut about it, because I did not want others to think I was crazy.

A few years back I was hunting in Buffalo County, Wisconsin in mid-October and enjoyed one of the most amazing mornings of buck activity that I have ever experienced. Later, I told my friend Tom Indrebo, about it. Tom might not have a degree in wildlife biology, but he knows more about whitetail deer than most wildlife professionals. As I told my story, Tom listened and just smiled. He had known about the October mini-rut for years. Since then, I have found a number of hunters who make it a point to be in the woods on these dates. Granted, the October mini-rut is not widespread. It appears to me that there are just a few old

Acorns are a big draw during the October Lull. The reason many hunters are not seeing deer is that the deer do not have to travel far from their bedding cover to begin munching on acorns.

Remember those food plots you put in last spring? Now is the time to make them pay off.

does that come into estrous a month early. But as you can imagine, those few does can attract a lot of attention.

HUNTING RUB LINES

Early and mid-October is a good time to be perched in a stand along a rub line. Not all of the bucks have gotten in on the rubbing action yet, so there is a good chance that the rub line you find now is the handiwork of the area's dominant buck. As strange as it sounds, the rubs are not really the reason I hunt rub lines at this time of the year. I know that a buck is not inclined to return to a specific rub.

But I also know that a rub line nearly always indicates the travel route a buck is taking between bedding and feeding sites, and that is some important information.

WHAT ABOUT SCRAPES?

Most hunters do not start looking for scrape action until the end of October or first week of November. That is because scrapes are easy to find then. The reason they are so easy to find is that anything with antlers jutting through the noggin is getting in on the dirt-throwing action. Nothing wrong with that, unless of course, you have your heart set on a better-than-average buck. The best time to catch a big buck working scrapes is before all of the other deer start scraping. Dominant bucks will be pawing out scrapes at least a week before other bucks and I've often seen them start two weeks earlier. It takes some detective work, but if you can find those mid-October scrapes, they are worth hunting over.

MOCK SCRAPES

I start putting in mock scrapes in the spring. You might think that is awful early to be putting in mock scrapes. After all, the bucks do not even have antlers yet. But after a lot of years of messing around with mock scrapes, I have found that there is no such thing as too early, only too late, when it comes to mock scrapes. Most hunters don't use mock scrapes until they begin to see real scrapes in the woods. By then you have lost the advantage. Now your mock scrapes have to compete with an ever increasing number of real scrapes. But if you make them early (I make most of mine in July, August and early September), bucks will find some of them and be in the habit of visiting them long before serious scraping begins. That is a huge advantage.

Making mock scrapes is easy. Use a garden trowel and clear a small oval or round shape under an overhanging branch. If there is no overhanging branch where you want to make the mock scrape, just secure a branch from another tree so that it hangs about five feet above where you want to make the mock scrape. Hang a scent wick from the branch and apply any scent containing forehead gland to the branch tip and the wick. Work your favorite scent into the scrape and bury a BucRut scent wafer an inch or two under the surface. The scent wafer will ooze odor up through the dirt for a long time. Often I have had bucks paw the scent wafer out of the ground. Pour a cup of Primetime Magic Scrape into the center of the mock scrape. Make a depression in the center of the mound of Magic Scrape and fill it with your favorite scent. That's it. I have found over the years that mock scrapes are most effective if I make a mock scrape line instead of a single mock scrape.

THE ACORN DROP

One of the reasons why so many bowhunters give up on mid-October hunting is that whitetail deer often will suddenly abandon the fields in which hunters have been seeing them feed each evening. These hunters mistakenly believe that these deer have gone nocturnal. But most of the time, that is not the case. The deer are still feeding each evening (and in the morning as well), but they have just switched restaurants. Often acorns are the big draw at this time. Instead of dashing right out into the fields to feed, deer munch acorns for an hour or so and then wander out into the fields for a little dessert. When deer quit coming to your favorite field, don't give up and quit hunting until November. Just start snooping around in the timber for places where the acorns are dropping. The odds are pretty good you will find your deer.

KEEP TABS ON THE CROP HARVEST

Along the same lines, it pays to keep tabs on the crop harvest. For example, deer are very attracted to a harvested cornfield. Mechanical pickers leave plenty of waste corn and deer are quick to arrive on the scene to take advantage of it. With the big machinery many farmers use today, it is not unusual for a farmer to pick a field one day and have it plowed under just a few days later. That means you need to stay on top of the harvest to take advantage of these often narrow windows of opportunity.

DON'T FORGET THE WATER

Because the weather is often on the warm side in early and mid-October, hunting over or near ponds, seeps and creeks where deer drink is a good option. If I had my own farm, the first thing I would do is put in a secluded pond or two. Deer are just like you and I when it comes to drinking: the warmer the weather the more fluids we need. In warm weather deer will usually drink shortly after getting up in the evening and before turning in for the morning. But it is not unusual for them to grab a drink in late morning or early afternoon as well. Being secretive

creatures, deer prefer to drink in secretive locations. For example, if a deer has a choice between drinking from a muddy little pond tucked deep in protective cover or exposing itself to drink from the creek which twists through the pasture, the deer will happily drink at the muddy little pond.

HUNT THE BEDROOM

There is no question that deer spend most of the daylight hours bedded at this time of the season. That is why it is important that you know where the deer bed. Sometimes you can figure it out with just tracks, trails and a knowledge of where the heaviest cover is on the property you hunt. But sometimes you just have to start walking the best cover until you start jumping deer. Don't worry, deer won't abandon a bedding area just because you disturb them. Once you know where the deer bed, pick a couple of good stand locations right on the edge of the bedding cover, put up your stands and then get out.

No, October is not as action-packed as the November rut. But deer do not crawl into a hole and hide come October. And unless they have been heavily pressured, they don't go strictly nocturnal either. Deer are still doing what deer do. Don't let all of the misinformation about the so-called "October Lull" keep you out of the woods this October.

Looking for scrapes in mid-October will help to locate big dominant bucks.

Chapter Seven

∽∾

CALLING & RATTLING

Regardless of the time of the season, you will not find me in the woods without a deer call or two, and either a set of rattling antlers or a rattling bag in my possession. No, I do not use them every time out. Sometimes I go for days without doing any rattling or calling. But when I need them, I want them handy. Like the time I was perched in a big oak on the edge of a strip of river-bottom timber. Deer were traveling that river bottom between bedding areas in a large woods to the north and a lush alfalfa field a mile to the south. There was a trail seventeen yards from the tree in which I perched that looked like it had been pounded out by a herd of cattle, but there were no cattle on that stretch of timber. The trail, devoid of all vegetation and worn an inch deep into the earth, was the work of the repeated pounding of deer hooves. I had already seen a dozen deer that morning. Most had been does and fawns, but there had been three small

A grunt call can help you turn those buck sightings into bucks on the ground.

bucks. All had traipsed right down that trail. But the stocky nine-pointer that came along just as the morning heat was making me consider calling it a morning was not on the trail. Instead he was walking across a CRP field 150 yards to my west, headed for the big timber to bed just like all of the other deer, but for whatever reason, just taking a different route. Without my grunt tube, I would have just had to watch him walk away, but I put the tube to my mouth and gave a single grunt.

It was early in the season, September 19th to be exact, and I have found the single note contact grunt to be the most reliable buck grunt to use early in the season. The buck was about as far away as I figured a deer could hear the low volume vocalization, even on a quiet morning like this one. But that single grunt stopped the buck in his tracks and he turned to stare in my direc-

Many gun hunters are under the mistaken impression that calling only works during the bow season, but there are many instances during the gun season when calling will work very well.

tion. I was tempted to grunt again, but deer are very good at pinpointing the exact location of any noise, so I resisted the urge to call again and waited.

With a flick of his tail, the buck turned and started walking in my direction. He never stopped walking until he was standing on that well-worn trail just a chip shot from my stand. The broadhead took him square behind the shoulders, the buck whirled, ran out into the CRP field and fell dead, all in less time than it took you to read this sentence.

Does a grunt tube always work magic like that? Of course not. I've had lots of bucks ignore my grunts. I've had others acknowledge that they heard them and then for whatever reason just decide not to investigate. But a grunt tube is a tool that I will not be without, because very often the ability to communicate with deer that are out of range has made the difference between a shot and no shot.

Early in the season I rely primarily on the contact grunt. It is a low volume, single note grunt, which is probably just one buck's way of asking if there are any other bucks in the area. In my experience, the contact grunt is effective about 50 percent of the time, which means that half of the deer which I grunt to using the contact grunt respond to the call. That, by the way, is a better average than I have been able to maintain using the more aggressive and certainly more well-known tending and trailing grunts common to the rut.

Whitetail deer are much more vocal than most hunters give them credit for.

I switch over to the trailing grunt, which is a louder, more repetitious grunt sometime in mid-October. Although you can call in bucks using the trailing grunt early in the season, I think you will find the contact grunt a better choice. During post-rut, I do very little calling. Bucks are worn out now and in my experience they are very reluctant to come to the call. I don't want to educate them by calling to them when they are unlikely to respond, so I just do not call much during the post-rut.

But by late season, I pick up the action again. Sometimes I go with a trailing or tending grunt, other times I use the contact grunt. I think the edge goes to the contact grunt during the late season. I've called in deer during September, October, November, December and January. Most of them were deer which I would never have had the opportunity to shoot if not for calling. That is reason enough for me to make sure that I have grunt call with me each time I go hunting. In fact, I usually have an extra in my fanny pack and a couple of spares in my truck.

DOE CALLS

It was the middle of October, but it was obvious that the buck I was watching was definitely out looking for does. That did not surprise me much. Deer don't follow a calendar nearly as closely as we hunters do. The buck was halfway across the clear-cut when

I first spotted him. Nose to the ground, he was walking at a fast pace like bucks do when they are frantically trying to cut the track of a hot doe. I hit him with a series of grunts first, but he never indicated that he heard them. He was just a tad over 100 yards away, pretty close for rattling, but I had to do something, so I grabbed the horns and clattered them together.

That did it. The buck skidded to a halt, threw his head high and stared in my direction. He wanted to hear more, but I did not dare give it to him. I knew if I moved that the buck would see me. For maybe 20 seconds he stared hard and then with a quick twitch of his tail, he lowered his head and continued on his way. I brought the horns together again, but the buck never broke stride. He had had his look. In desperation I grabbed the grunt tube again. This time I depressed the reed with my trigger finger and sent the wailing moan of a doe bleat out across the clear-cut.

The buck liked that. He stopped and stared again. I don't like to call again when a buck is looking my way, but I knew that if I did not do something, that this one would likely continue on his way again, so I depressed the reed on the True-Talker and hit him with another doe bleat. That did it. Without hesitation the buck headed my way, walking at first and then breaking into a trot. I sent an arrow zipping through his chest at about eight

yards. Not bad for a guy who used to scoff at doe calls. I'll be the first to admit that for many years I relied only on buck vocalizations when calling deer. I saw no need for doe vocalizations. In fact, I considered the so-called doe bleat or estrous bleat to be a hoax. I spend as much time in the whitetail woods as anyone I know, but only rarely had I heard a doe bleat and when I did it had always been the soft bleat a doe uses when communicating with it's fawn.

I reasoned that if a doe really did bleat, in estrous or out, I would have heard it numerous times. But that is not the case. In the last few years, I have heard does bleat loudly on three different occasions. In all three cases the doe doing the bleating was being pursued by an amorous buck. Even that does not, in my mind, confirm that the bleats had anything to do with an urgent need to be bred, as some call manufactures suggest. In fact, because in each case the does seemed to be doing their best to give the buck the slip, my guess is that the bleat was more out of fear or perhaps annoyance than any signal of an urgency to breed. So while I remain unconvinced about the validity of the estrous bleat, I am no longer skeptical of the effectiveness of the vocalization. It has worked for me on too many occasions in the past few years for me to any longer remain skeptical.

Odds are, I will never know if a buck recognizes the doe bleat as a signal that there is a doe in desperate need of his services or

A good variable tone grunt call will allow you to make not only buck grunts, but also doe bleats that can be very effective at the right time.

not. The truth is, it is not really important to me that I know. It is enough that I know that the doe bleat does get results. I guess that is the difference between a researcher and a hunter. There are a number of ways to use a doe bleat to your advantage. The most common method I employ when hunting specifically for bucks is to mix a few doe bleats in with tending or trailing grunts. It would go something like this: uurrrrp–uuurrrp-uurrp–blaaah–uuurrrrp-uuurrp-uuurrrp-blaaaahh——uuurrrp. You can mix it up anyway you like and choose to go with as few as a half dozen buck grunts with only one or two doe bleats mixed in, or, as I sometimes do, let it roll on for twenty or more grunts with a half-dozen doe bleats scattered throughout the calling sequence.

Calling deer is not an exact science, so

When calling blind, keep an arrow nocked.
A buck could show up at any time.

have fun with it, experiment, find out what works best for you. Of course I would never be so bold as to assume that I know how a buck's brain works, but my guess is that when a buck hears a series of buck grunts punctuated with doe bleats, that the buck is smart enough to know that there is darn sure a buck carrying on with a doe on the other side of the ridge.

If the buck that hears the vocalizations is not in the company of a doe, or if he is not still licking his wounds from just having been thoroughly whipped by a bigger, nastier buck, there is a good chance that the buck will wander over to see about stealing the doe away. As you might suspect, there is no way in which I can prove that mixing a few doe bleats in with my buck grunts makes the calling more effective. But I believe that it does and that is good enough for me. Nothing beats confidence when it comes to calling critters and I have a lot of confidence in this calling strategy.

Some hunters of my acquaintance have had good luck calling bucks by using the doe bleat without the buck grunts. I have not enjoyed that same success, even though I have tried it a lot. The buck in the beginning of this story was the exception, not the rule, in my own case. I do not doubt that the many hunters who have told me of calling in bucks with doe bleats are telling me the truth. None are call manufactures, so they had nothing to gain by trying to deceive me. I will continue

Don't overdo it when calling during the late season. Remember, those bucks have heard it all by this time of year.

to experiment, but since I have had such good results by mixing doe bleats with my buck grunts, I am sure I will rely upon that strategy more than any other.

If you, on the other hand, have enjoyed good success using a doe bleat solo, by all means stick with it. If you are going to mix a few doe bleats in with your tending or trailing grunts, there are two methods for accomplishing that goal. One is to use a good variable tone grunt call. It must be a call that you can switch from a buck grunt to a doe bleat without taking the call apart.

There are many excellent variable tone grunt calls on the market that you must take apart in order to change the rubber band to the appropriate position on the reed for the tone you desire. These calls will not work for blending doe bleats with buck grunts simply because it takes too long to alter them.

You could buy two and leave one set on buck grunt and the other on doe bleat, but I don't know why you would do that when one good variable tone grunt tube is really all you need. The call I use most often is a True-Talker and it is about as simple as it gets. Blow it and you get an excellent buck grunt, depress the reed with a little finger pressure and you have a great doe bleat.

Another option is to use the hand-operated cylinder calls manufactured by Primos, Quaker Boy and Hunter's Specialties. There are three different sizes of canister: a small one for close range work, one for medium distances and another larger can for long range calling. All of these work the same way. Tip them over and when you bring them right side up, the cylinder emits a very good doe bleat. With one of these in your hand, it is easy to mix a few bleats in with your grunts, no matter what kind of grunt tube you prefer.

FAWN BLEATS FOR THE EARLY SEASON

The first deer I killed this past archery season was a fat doe which came to a fawn-in-distress vocalization. You can make the bawling sound of a fawn in trouble on some variable tone grunt calls, but a fawn bleat call, which is usually used by predator hunters for calling coyotes, does a better job. On that warm, humid evening in late September, I was looking to fill one of my antlerless archery tags.

Our oldest daughter and her family were out of venison, a situation we just cannot tolerate in the Clancy family. Nothing seemed to be moving that evening, so about a half hour before dark, I raised the call and cut loose with a series of six or eight fawn bleats, with a pause of maybe five to ten seconds between each bleat. The doe showed up maybe a minute after the sound of the last bleat had faded. It was obvious that the doe was looking for the source of the sound.

When she walked past my stand at about fifteen yards she presented a very easy broadside shot. I'm sure that does respond to the doe bleat early in the season because they think the sound is made by a fawn in distress. Often when a doe comes in to a fawn bleat she is agitated and anxious. You might call in a doe with a fawn bleat call at any time during the season, but in my experience they are most effective during September and the first half of October. Later in the season, the maternal instinct does not seem to be as strong. You also want to be ready for multiple deer responding to the fawn bleat. I'm not sure why this occurs, but I suspect it is a matter of the entire family

Bleats and doe grunts are too soft to be of much use when it comes to calling deer to you, but they are great for settling down deer that are nervous.

unit responding to a distress cry. Whatever the reason, there have been a number of times when I have had several does all come running at once.

SOFT BLEATS & DOE GRUNTS

Soft bleats, as the name suggests, are very low volume bleats. Doe grunts are also very subdued when compared to a buck grunt. Neither can be heard at a very long distance. In my experience, under ideal conditions a deer can hear either the soft bleat or the doe grunt at only 40 to 60 yards. Does use both the soft

bleat and the doe grunt to communicate with other deer, mainly their fawns and daughters from previous years which have become part of the doe family unit. I do not rely on either vocalization to call deer, but I know how to make both of them and have used them quite often to help settle deer down which have heard or seen something (usually me) which has made them nervous. It is really quite amazing how a hyper doe will settle down and relax after hearing a few soft bleats or doe grunts. Sometimes, if there is a buck lurking nearby, being able to diffuse a potentially explosive problem can pay big dividends.

Are doe vocalizations as important in deer hunting as the more commonly used buck vocalizations? In my experience, the answer to that would be no, they are not. But on the other hand, I have to admit that doe vocalizations are certainly far more important than I once gave them credit for.

I like a versatile call that will allow me to make buck grunts and doe bleats with the same call.

Anyone who is not capable of reproducing the doe bleat is probably missing out on some action as a result.

WHAT ABOUT RATTLING?

The peak period for rattling is that ten-day to two-week long stretch commonly called late pre-rut. It's those days right before does start coming into estrous in numbers great enough to occupy most of the bucks. During this period, bucks are so super-charged on an overdose of the hormone testosterone that is not uncommon for them to come to the sound of clashing antlers on a dead run.

One foggy morning while bow-hunting on Willow Point, an island in the Mississippi between the states of Louisiana and Mississippi, I had just finished a short rattling session and hung up my rattling horns when I heard a buck coming on the run from behind me. I grabbed my bow and turned just as the buck, a six-point, skidded to halt right under the spreading oak in which I perched.

Nearly at the same instant, another buck dashed in and stopped on the other side of the tree. Then a third buck, slightly bigger than the first two, bolted out of the fog and also put on the brakes right under the tree. For an instant all three bucks just stared at each other, and then, as if on que, they all turned and raced away. It all happened so quick that I was left wondering if it had ever really happened, but my shaking right leg left no doubt that it had. Rattling isn't always that productive or exciting, but it can be.

I know that most hunters would never consider rattling early in the season. That I think, is a mistake. Rattling now is not nearly as effective as it is during the latter stages of pre-rut and the first leg of the rut itself, but it's darn sure a tactic to keep in mind when the situation calls for it. I've rattled in a number of bucks in September and early October. I've even had bucks which were still in velvet come to the horns while rattling in early September. I'll admit that surprised me, although it probably should not have.

Whitetail deer are curious critters. Even though those bucks were certainly not looking for a fight, their curiosity was aroused. And hey, I don't really care what makes them respond, just so long as they respond. Early in the season bucks do a lot of antler tickling and light sparring with each other. A rattling bag does an excellent job of imitating the clickety-clickety-clack of tine tickling. I've found that if I hear a couple of bucks doing some light sparring back in the timber, if I wait for a break in the action and then do a little clicking of my own on the rattle bag, most of the time at least one of the bucks, and often both of them, will come in to investigate. Usually

it is the small bucks that respond, but on occasion I have had bigger bucks respond.

From about the middle of October right on through the main rut I rely mainly on a big set of rattling antlers and do a lot of rattling. Rattling is much more productive in some parts of the country than in others, but this has nothing to do with latitude and longitude and everything to do with herd dynamics.

In a nutshell, rattling response will be greatest in places where the buck-to-doe ratio is as close to one-to-one as possible. Rattling is best in areas where mature bucks make up a reasonable percentage of the buck population. Competition is what spurs rattling action. During post-rut and late season I have had very poor results with rattling. In fact, I've run off so many bucks while trying to entice them with rattling, that I have just about quit rattling during the period all together. I still carry a rattle bag with me just in case, but I use it only when I have a buck in sight that has ignored my grunts and doe bleats and is not going to come closer on his own. Then I have nothing to lose by trying to entice him with a little light rattling. But like I said, all I've accomplished is to run most of these deer off.

Rattling and calling are two techniques which should be included in every hunters bag of tricks. No, they do not work every time, but they certainly work often enough that you are missing out on some action if you are not using them.

Chapter Eight

❧

SCENTING
SCRAPES

I am a big fan of tuning-up scrapes, but despite the success I've enjoyed hunting over them, I won't sit here and try to convince you that all you have to do to see more bucks and bigger bucks is to pour some pee in a scrape and get ready for a buck parade. It does not work that way. I've carefully scented a lot of scrapes and then hunted over them without ever seeing a buck. So why bother? Because over the past 20 years I have had more bucks visit scrapes which I have doctored-up with scent than have visited scrapes which have not been tuned-up. I believe that the biggest advantage you gain from adding scent to scrapes and overhanging branches is that the scent you add triggers a response from any buck visiting the scrape. Perhaps that response is one of aggression or dominance if buck urine or tarsal gland scent is used. It may trigger sexual frustration if a doe-in-estrous urine is employed. Or maybe all scents simply trigger the natural

When doctoring existing scrapes or mock scrapes,
be generous with the scent you use.

curiosity of the whitetail. This, I believe, certainly helps explain why researchers have sometimes found bucks to be attracted to scrapes which have been tainted with human urine. Ultimately I don't care what is going through the buck's mind when he pays that visit. All I care about is making sure that if a buck is going to visit a scrape during shooting hours, that the scrape he selects is the one I'm sitting over. Deer remember where they found things that smelled or tasted good to them. That is what keeps them coming back to that apple tree each evening. If you can make a buck remember that he smelled something good in a certain scrape, then you are on your way to accomplishing that goal.

HOW TO TUNE UP A SCRAPE

When I first began messing around with deer scents and later adding scents to scrapes, deciding what scent to use was easy. All we had was what we called "doe pee." Today, there are over 100 choices on the market. Scents based on deer urine are still the biggest sellers, but many have now added tarsal gland, interdigital gland and even forehead gland to the mix. Synthetics are big too.

The so-called "solid scents," the pastes, gels, crystals and pellets, will probably dominate the scent industry one day. I have not used them all, but I have tested a lot of them and although I have had better results with some than others, I would not conclude that my in-the-field tests really prove anything. If a buck happens to visit a scrape I've tuned-up with product A on Monday but I don't see a buck while hunting over a scrape juiced up with product B on Tuesday, does it mean that product A is more attractive to bucks than product B?

Everything you need for making mock scrapes or doctoring scrapes.

I don't think so. Instead I pick my "favorites" using a different criteria.

How long does a buck hang around when he visits one of my tuned-up scrapes? If a buck spends a lot of time sniffing and licking at the scrape and overhanging branch, then I figure the scent I used has really got his attention. I've had bucks spend over ten minutes at scrapes I've scented. One Illinois buck came back to visit a scrape I was sitting over six times in one day. You can bet that the scent I was using in that scrape is on my all-time-favorites list.

More important than what brand of scent you leave behind at the scrape is the brand of scent you do not leave behind. I'm talking about human odor of course. When I tune-up a scrape I wear a Scent-Lok suit, rubber boots (often hip-boots) and rubber gloves. A mature buck lives by his nose and if his nose tells him that a human has been at his scrape, then I don't care what brand of scent you use, odds are good that buck will never visit that scrape again. To tune-up a scrape I begin by using a stick or a garden trowel to work up the soil in the scrape. Usually I work in some gel or paste lure at the same time. If it is a scrape that I know I might not be able to hunt for several days, I bury an H.S. BucRut wafer an inch under the soil or I take a small jar or 35mm film canister, add scent, poke some holes in the lid and bury it an inch or so under the surface. Next I pour a large handful of Magic Scrape into the center of the

The overhanging branch is the real communication center at any scrape.

scrape. Magic Scrape is a specially blended, waterproof soil that bucks find very attractive by itself but I spice it up a little by making a depression in the mound of Magic Scrape and adding a half ounce of liquid scent. That's it for the scrape, now onto the really important stuff: the overhanging branch. Every scrape worth hunting over has an overhanging branch and it is here that the real scent communication between deer takes place. Many times I have watched deer come into a scrape and never even bother to sniff the scrape itself, but spend minutes licking, chewing, rubbing their faces on and hooking the overhanging branch with their antlers. A buck leaves scent behind from his tarsal, saliva, forehead, nasal, and pre-orbital glands as well as his urine when he works an overhanging branch. Add a little of your favorite scent to the branch itself and then take a scent wick and secure it to the branch with wire or a plastic tie. Don't be cheap when it comes to applying scent to that scent wick, soak it until it won't hold anymore.

NOT ALL SCRAPES ARE CREATED EQUAL

When I first began hunting over scrapes I only had one criteria in choosing the scrape I hunted over: Size. The bigger the better I figured. The problem with really big scrapes, or community scrapes as they are commonly called (because these huge scrapes are nearly always the work of more than one buck), is that they are usually found on the edge of a major feeding location—which in most whitetail habitats is spelled f-i-e-l-d. Does gather here each night to feed. Bucks come to sniff the does. One buck walks over and paws out a scrape. As soon as he walks off another steps up to the plate and then the next and the next and the next.

My friend Tom Indrebo once placed a Cam Trakker near such a scrape. In a single night all 24 exposures fired. We checked the prints with an 8X lupe to make sure we did not count the same

buck twice and came up with an astounding nineteen different bucks visiting that scrape in one night. That's how you get a "community scrape."

The problem with these big scrapes is that all of the action takes place at night. On rare occasions, when the testosterone is peaking in a mature buck's system, that buck may become so bold as to visit such a scrape during shooting hours, but I don't want to bet on those odds. Instead, I look for scrapes in or near heavy cover; the kind of places a big buck is going to lay up in for part of the day. I want the scrape I tune-up to be accessible to that buck. A scrape in such a location gives me an excellent chance of intercepting the buck as he enters his bedding area in early morning or as he exits in late afternoon.

A tuned-up scrape in heavy cover is also one of my favorite places to pull an all day sit, something I do quite often during the late pre-rut. Most deer get up out of their beds at mid-day to relieve themselves, stretch and browse a little. Big bucks are no exception. Many times, when the scraping phase is in full-swing, a buck will check a nearby scrape or two during this mid-day activity period; "nearby" is the key word here.

TIMING YOUR TUNE-UP

You will often read that the peak scraping period of the rut occurs during the two weeks prior to the first does entering estrous, and this information is accurate. During this two-week long stretch every

Bucks, like this western Illinois Droptine, may make 100 or more scrapes before he is done. A little scent in the scrapes nearest your stand will encourage him to pay those scrapes a visit.

buck in the timber gets into the scraping mode. The problem with this period is that if you are hunting an area with a decent buck population, there are too many scrapes. With so many scrapes it is more difficult to elicit interest in your tuned-up scrape. Also, when scraping is at it's peak it is nearly impossible to concentrate your efforts on a mature buck.

That is why my favorite time to tune-up scrapes is before the late pre-rut period. Mature bucks begin scraping earlier, often as much as two weeks earlier, than immature bucks. Finding a big buck's scrapes takes some snooping, but I have found it to be worth the effort. I stick with adding scent to scrapes and hunting over scrapes right up until the bucks start chasing the does. Once that action starts there are better places to hunt, but until that happens a tuned-up scrape can really tune-up your season.

THE SCOOP ON MOCK SCRAPES
Halloween 1988 was a nasty day for the little trick-or-treaters. It was cold, but not

quite cold enough for the light rain, which had fallen all morning, to turn to snow. I had been in a tree stand, located on an oak-studded ridge, not far outside Lanesboro, since before first light. By mid-morning, I was pretty darn miserable. At noon, a hot meal down at the Chat-and-Chew was sounding mighty tempting.

I just kept reminding myself that over the years I have seen a lot of nice bucks right around Halloween. Many of them have showed up during the middle of the day. So I munched a soggy peanut butter sandwich and waited. An hour later I saw him. A fine eight-point buck working his way down the old logging road towards my perch. Twice the buck stopped to work scrapes along the road. That did not surprise me, because I had made those scrapes months earlier.

As the buck finished the second scrape and continued down the logging trail, I let him walk just past my stand to where I had placed a mock scrape in a perfect position so that any buck working the scrape would present me with an easy shot from my tree stand. Predictably the buck stopped at the mock scrape and when he lifted his head to work the overhanging branch, I drew, picked my spot and released. Everything about that encounter, including the shot, was picture perfect. That stout eight-pointer was the first buck I ever took over a mock scrape, but he would not be the last.

During the past fifteen years I've killed other bucks that have been attracted to my mock scrapes and let dozens of young

bucks walk. There is no such thing as a magic potion when it comes to whitetail hunting, but mock scrapes are close. Mock scrapes have been around a long, long time. The reason for that longevity is that mock scrapes work. No, they do not work every time, nothing does in the world of whitetail hunting, but they darn sure work often enough that this whitetail addict spends a few days each summer making mock scrapes. If you want to up your odds of seeing a good buck at point-blank range this fall, you might consider doing the same.

I start making my mock scrapes in July and August. You might be thinking that this is a little early to be making mock scrapes. After all, the bucks are still in velvet and will not be scraping in earnest until mid-October. But trust me, this is not too early. I have found that the earlier you make mock scrapes the better the response rate.

In fact, the biggest mistake you can make when it comes to mock scrapes is to wait until the bucks start scraping before you make mock scrapes. By then, it is too late. Wait until then and you must compete with the real deal. But if you get those mock scrapes out there now, you are the first buck scraping in the neighborhood. Odds are good that you are going to get the attention of any buck that encounters the mock scrape. I always strive to be the first "buck" out there making scrapes. When a buck finds your mock scrapes, what you are hoping is that he begins to pay regular visits to them. Maybe he returns because he is looking for the intruder buck which made the mock scrape. Or maybe, as commonly happens, the buck just takes the scrape over as one of his own and wants to keep it fresh.

Then again, it might be just the whitetail's inherent curiosity. Personally, I really don't much care why a buck pays repeated visits to a mock scrape. It is enough for me to know that they do.

Most mock scrapes attract the atten-

Spending a few days in the summer making mock scrapes can really pay off big in the fall.

Bucks spend a lot of time working overhanging branches. You can encourage them to hang around a little longer by doctoring branches near your stand.

tion of more than one buck. In good whitetail habitat, it is not unusual to have a half dozen or more bucks overlapping each other's home areas. All of the bucks will likely be attracted to your mock scrapes. That really boosts the odds that you are going to catch one of them in the act come hunting season. Your best chance of doing just that is going to occur in late pre-rut. Many hunters make the mistake of sticking with hunting over mock scrapes or real scrapes after there are estrous does on the scene. Usually, this is a waste of time because buck visits to mock scrapes drop off precipitously when the breeding starts.

Of course there are a lot of factors that dictate when and how often a buck will visit a mock scrape. Hunting pressure is a big one. If hunting pressure is heavy, as it usually is on opening weekend of the firearms season, it is unlikely that a buck is going to come strolling along checking scrapes. But just as soon as the number of hunters slacks off, bucks will get right back to business.

Weather has something to do with it too. Cold fronts are best for good buck activity. Warm

Cooler weather will lead to an increase in buck movement. I took this buck on the morning a cold front moved in.

weather tends to shut down daytime activity. But if a cold front is forecast on the heels of a warmer than average spell, call in sick and get to the woods. The bucks will be on the prowl big time. Ditto for a day which features a light rain or falling snow.

Herd composition is another major fac-tor. You will have your best response rate at mock scrapes in areas with a reasonably balanced buck-to-doe ratio and a number of mature bucks in the buck population. Sadly, there are many areas in the country where you have neither working in your favor. If you are not getting any response to your mock scrapes, it probably is not that you are doing anything wrong, it is just that the herd dynamics in your area are not conducive to good results with mock scrapes.

Accept the fact that most of the activity at your mock scrapes is going to occur at night. Researchers have determined that about 75 percent of all scraping activity takes place under cover of darkness. Some hunters tend to focus on the 75 percent and figure that making mock scrapes and hunting over them is just not worth the effort. I prefer to look at the other 25 percent. Those are good enough odds for me.

LOCATION IS EVERYTHING

As in real estate, location is everything when it comes to mock scrapes. You want to make your mock scrapes easy to find. That means making mock scrapes along trails and edges where bucks travel. If you know where bucks have left scrapes in other seasons, make your mock scrapes in the same area. The key is to make the mock scrapes impossible to miss.

MAKING THE MOCK SCRAPE

Human scent around the mock scrape is not good. Sure the human scent will dissipate in time, but what if Mr. Big visits before then and get's a whiff of you? Think he will come back later to check out the mock scrape? Fat chance. I wear clean clothes, rubber boots and gloves when I make mock scrapes. The most important part of a mock scrape is the overhanging branch. The branch should hang about five feet above the ground. If there is not a branch where you plan to make a scrape, you can cut one and attach it where you want it.

Hang a scent wick from the branch and apply scent to the scent wick and the branch itself. When a buck works an overhanging branch he leaves a mixture of scent from his pre-orbital glands, nasal glands, saliva glands, forehead glands and tarsal glands. Any scent which contains all or any of these glandular secretions will work just fine.

A very good one is very appropriately named Lick'N Stick. Beneath the branch, use a garden trowel to clear a patch of bare earth. Don't get carried away. All you need to do is get the scrape started, visiting bucks will enlarge it. I dig a hole a couple of inches deep and bury a Buc-Rut Scent Wafer in the hole. Then I pour a cup of Primetime Magic Scrape into the scrape and add a little of my favorite liquid or gel scent to the mound of Magic Scrape.

I've found that while a single mock scrape will get some attention, a line or string of mock scrapes along a trail or the top of a ridge is much better. Bucks seem to get in the habit of checking out the whole string. If you have not tried mock scrapes, give them a try this season. They are easy to make and work very well if you have mature bucks in the area you hunt. And it's pretty darn neat watching a buck work a scrape that you have made.

Serious odor control means spraying down everything with an odor neutralizer.

Chapter Nine

❦

DECOYING &
USING SCENTS

No matter where you hunt, if there are whitetails around, they can be enticed to pay a decoy a visit. It does not matter if you hunt a small patchwork of woodlots and farm fields, riverbottoms, the suburbs or the big timber; decoying will work. When it comes to decoying deer, placement and positioning of the decoy are vital to success. So are factors like visibility, timing, odor control and finally, choosing the right decoy for your style of hunting. Let's start with how to position your decoy, because this is one of the biggest mistakes I see hunters make when using a decoy. In all cases the wind should be blowing from the decoy to your stand or at the very worst a cross-wind. Attempting to hunt over a decoy with the breeze blowing from you to the decoy, no matter how careful you are about odor control, is just asking for trouble. My decoy is never more than 20 yards from

I do not use a decoy as often when hunting before or after the rut as I do during the rut. However, each season there are situations that call for the use of a decoy when hunting prior to or after the rut.

Laying down a scent trail won't do you any good if you are laying down a trail of human scent at the same time. Wear clean boots and spray down your boots and pants legs with a good odor neutralizer before hiking into your stand.

my stand and often much closer. I do this so that if a buck hangs up beyond the decoy, which a few are going to do, chances are good that the deer will still be within my range. When using a buck decoy, face the decoy towards the stand. The reason for this is when a buck approaches a buck decoy, it will nearly always circle around the decoy and come in head-to-head or at least head-to-shoulder.

This is probably a natural defense mechanism on the part of the buck. My guess is that the buck wants to keep an eye on the antlers of the other buck because those are the potentially lethal weapons. If the decoy is facing your position, a buck will usually provide you with a perfect broadside or quartering shot.

With a doe decoy, you want to have the decoy either facing directly away or quartering away. A buck will nearly always approach a doe decoy from the rear because that is the end of the doe he is most interested in. If I have to explain that any further, you are probably reading the wrong book!

Maximum visibility is crucial to success when using a decoy. The further away a buck can spot your decoy the better the odds that he will commit to your decoy. Field edges are ideal locations for a decoy. So are sloughs, clear-cuts, cut-lines and fence-lines. A decoy will work just fine when hunting open stands of mature timber, or woods that have been pastured so that the undergrowth is not too thick. But in heavy cover, where a deer is going to be right on top of the decoy before it can see the decoy, a decoy will cost you opportunities. I've seen bucks turn tail and run like the wind when suddenly encountering a decoy at close range. I wonder if they do that when they suddenly come upon a real deer?

Because whitetail deer are social creatures, a deer might investigate a decoy at any time during the season. I've used them successfully from September through January. However, the most consistent action over a decoy will occur during the ten-day to two-week long stretch just prior to the first wave of does coming into estrous. It is at this time that bucks will go out of their way to investigate grunt calls and rattling which I commonly use to draw a buck's attention to the decoy.

Don't rule out using a decoy during the early weeks of the season or during late season hunts. Under the right circumstances, a decoy can be a huge factor at any time of the season. The slightest trace of human odor on the decoy will spook a deer. To prevent contaminating my decoys with human odor I wear rubber or heavy, clean canvas gloves when handling the decoy. Once the decoy is in position, I spray down the entire decoy with a liquid odor neutralizer. If you take these precautions and store your decoy where it will not become contaminated with odors like paint, smoke, cooking grease or diesel exhaust in the off season, you should not have any trouble.

Deer scent does not make a decoy any more attractive to deer, but I have found that the addition of scent will hold deer around your decoy a little longer. This gives you more time to make a good shot. I don't like to use scent directly on the decoy. Instead, I take a stick and jam it in the ground beneath the decoy. On the stick I hang an absorbent scent wick and

Visibility is crucial in the successful use of decoys. This group of decoys has been placed in an open area for maximum exposure. A buck is more likely to investigate a decoy that he can see from a distance than one encountered suddenly in thick cover.

apply the scent to the wick. I usually use a doe-in-estrous urine when using a doe decoy and a buck urine or tarsal gland scent when using a buck decoy. Some hunters like to rub a slice of apple or the meat of an acorn on the nose of their decoy for a little added attraction.

There are over a dozen decoys on the market today. Which of these decoys is right for you depends upon a number of factors. For most of us, cost is an issue. You can spend $25 or $1,000 on a decoy. Portability is another consideration. If you are going to be hiking long distances to reach the places where you can use your decoy, you don't want a 3D decoy. Silhouettes are the way to go if this is your circumstance. No, silhouettes are not as effective as full-bodied decoys, but they are a whole lot more effective than you might think. I use them a lot when I hike into distant stands. But if I can drive near to or right up to my stand with an ATV or my pickup, I'll go with a full-body. If I will be hunting in the evening I'll try to drive in and drop off my decoys at mid-day. If I'm hunting the morning, I'll take them in the day before and stash the decoy in a deadfall or brush pile.

You might not shoot a bigger buck because you hunt with a decoy. You may not even see more deer in range, although I suspect that you will. But you will have a lot of fun watching deer interact with your decoy. There have been times when the antics of deer associating with my decoy have had me laughing so hard that I thought I was going to fall out of my tree stand. Hunting with a decoy is one of the the best ways I know to add a lot of enjoyment to the hunt.

DEER SCENTS

We have already covered how to use deer scents to enhance your decoy and how to doctor scrapes or make a mock scrape. There are however, a couple of other ways in which using deer scent may prove beneficial to your hunting success. Using scent wicks and laying down a scent trail are both time-tested and proven tactics that will work during early season, pre-rut and late season hunts.

I've proven to my satisfaction on dozens of occasions that using scent wicks can help hold a buck's attention while you draw your bow or move your rifle into position to make the shot. To me, that is reason enough for using scent wicks. Scent wicks also perform two other valuable functions. As the odor drifts downwind, any buck intercepting that odor is likely to follow his nose to the source.

This means that scent impregnated scent wicks probably will result in you seeing some deer which you likely otherwise would never lay eyes on. And third, scent bombs can help to cover up human odor, although I must caution you, that scent wicks will not make up for a lack of odor control on your part. Because I have deployed hundreds, probably thousands

It is rare that I hunt from a stand without first hanging a few scent wicks doctored with a favorite scent around my stand. I consider scent wicks to be a cheap insurance policy.

of scent bombs and scent wicks over the past 30 years and have yet to have buck number one spook from a scent wick, it is very rare that I do not deploy a few scent wicks around my stand. The only negative response to scent wicks that I have ever witnessed have been from does. On occasion I have had a doe being trailed by a buck become nervous when she encountered the scent from one of my scent bombs and lead the buck away instead of towards my position. This, of course, is not the reaction we are hoping for, but this occurrence is rare enough that I do not consider it a viable reason for not using scent bombs.

Before the first scent bombs, I simply applied my deer urine or lure to a shoulder-high branch or onto the trunk of a tree. After a season or two of that, I began using cotton balls and a few years later, like other hunters I began stuffing cotton balls into empty 35mm film canisters. These were the original scent bombs and

When you hike to your stand pulling a drag rag, you are laying down a trail of scent and any buck crossing the scent trail will be likely to follow to your stand.

despite all of the various scent wicks and variations of the old scent bomb on the market today, if you are the cost conscious type you can make the old original scent bombs for pennies each (not counting the cost of the scent) and they still get the job done. If you decide to use the 35mm scent bomb, the most important thing to remember is to pluck the cotton up out of the canister to form a wick so that the breeze can get at the scent and carry it.

During the 1980s some hunters, including myself, began experimenting with tampons for use as scent bombs. They worked well and I suspect that the idea for scent wicks, which are the most popular of all the scent bombs on the market today, originated from that concept. These super absorbent wicks hold a lot of scent for a long time and because the entire surface is exposed to the air, that scent is easily transported on the slightest breeze.

Don't get hung up on some precise strategy when it comes to deploying your scent wicks. There is nothing scientific about this. I use between four and eight wicks and arrange them in a circle around my stand when I am bowhunting, making sure that all of the scent wicks are within easy range of my stand. In fact, I often use the scent wicks as range markers.

All scent wicks should be hung in spots that you can shoot to if a buck is standing with his nose to the scent wick. Four to five feet is the perfect height at which to hang them. To avoid leaving any human scent on the wick, always wear gloves, preferably rubber gloves, whenever you handle the scent wicks. Be generous with the scent application. This is especially important when hunting for longer periods. The more scent you apply the longer it will take for the scent to evaporate and the better the odds that the scent wicks will still be working for you the entire time you are on stand.

When hunting with a gun, I often use scent wicks to encourage bucks to stop where I can get a good shot at them. I've deployed scent wicks more than 100 yards from my stand, hoping that the wick will stop a buck on a skinny logging road or along the edge of a natural woodland opening long enough for me to get off a good shot. This strategy has paid off often enough that I consider it to be well worth the effort.

Scent wicks are also a great way to use your favorite cover scent. Simply apply the cover scent to the wicks and hang two or three of them around you in your stand. When you are done hunting for the day, please take a minute and pick up all of your scent wicks. Put them in a Zip-Loc bag and they will be good to use the next time you hunt.

SCENT TRAILS

A scent trail will allow you to see deer that you otherwise would never have laid eyes on. The whole idea behind a scent trail is that when a buck cuts the trail, he will put his nose to the ground and follow it to your position. Does it work every time? Of course not. Nothing does in the world of whitetail hunting. But it darn sure works often enough that I have been a faithful scent trail maker for over 30 years. In fact, the biggest buck I have ever taken had his nose down on the scent trail I laid down that morning.

For most of that time I have relied on doe-in-estrous urine. I've tried other scents, including buck, doe and fawn urine, tarsal gland scent, a scent which incorporates interdigital gland and there

DECOYING & USING SCENTS

Stop every 50 yards as you hike to your stand and apply fresh scent to the drag rag to insure that the scent is getting stronger as you near your stand.

are times when I incorporate an interdigital gland scent with doe-in-estrous, but over the years, nothing has been as effective as a doe-in-estrous urine.

Doe-in-estrous scents are most effective during late pre-rut and the rut itself, but I do not hesitate to use a doe-in-estrous scent trail at anytime during the season. From the time a buck sheds his velvet until he casts his antlers he is capable of breeding and will likely find the smell of a doe-in-estrous to be at the very least, interesting. Laying down a scent trail is real easy, but there are two important considerations which will have a big influence on how receptive bucks are to your scent trails. One is the amount of scent you leave on the ground. Ideally you want the scent to remain constant or possibly even get stronger as you get closer to your

Make a whitetail's incredible sense of smell work for you, not against you.

This buck will go where his nose takes him.

stand. To accomplish this, I stop about every 50 yards and freshen up my drag rag. The other thing to be careful about is that there are not long gaps in your scent trail. A buck will lose interest really quick if he has to work to search for the next hint of scent.

Most of the advice you hear concerning scent trails suggests laying down a trail for only 100 or 200 yards. Me, I'm a believer in long-range scent trails. I've seen bucks follow a scent trail for 500 yards and I once backtracked a buck I killed on a scent trail after a fresh overnight snow and found that the buck had cut my scent trail just over 1,000 of my steps away from my stand. Whitetail deer are curious critters and even when the rut is not a major factor, bucks will follow a scent trail for a long way just out of curiosity. After all, unlike you and I who lead busy lives, that buck probably does not have anything better to do.

There is nothing scientific about laying down a scent trail. You have to walk into your stand anyway, so why not pull a drag rag behind you? You never know, like me, the biggest buck of your life may one day come sniffing his way along the scent trail you laid down.

Boot pads are one option for laying down a scent trail.

Chapter Ten

EARLY SEASON DEER DRIVES

Like many seasoned whitetail hunters, I have long suspected that the reason why so few mature bucks are killed on deer drives, even well-orchestrated drives, is that these deer just do not react or act like other deer. A mature buck has been around. He knows the drill. In the face of pressure, a mature buck rarely panics. A mature whitetail buck is Steven Segal, Harrison Ford, John Wayne and Steve McQueen all rolled into one. In short, he is one cool customer. But I have noticed that big bucks are more likely to make a mistake early in the season than they are later on, when being pushed around by hunters has become old hat to them. Of course that does not mean that a mature buck is a pushover early in the season. More of them will evade you than you will ever get your sights on. While hunting the

Ron Jolly and I are tickled with this
Mississippi nine-pointer.

September muzzleloader season in Kansas, I had a ringside seat which allowed me to see just how sneaky a big buck can be in the face of a well planned deer drive. There were six of us on that hunt. My old buddy J. Wayne Fears from Alabama, who has penned a couple of books for this publisher, Ken French, the head honcho at Thompson/Center and myself would do the posting. Our host, Rick Thompson, fellow writer Bryce Towsley and Ken's son Ernie would do the pushing. Both Bryce and Ernie had taken bucks earlier, which automatically gets you "doggin' duty" when deer drives are the order of the day. September may seem like a strange time to be putting on deer drives. After all, the deer are supposed to be coming out to feed each evening on lush alfalfa or the tender new growth on late-planted soybeans. They are supposed to be dependable in this late summer/ early autumn routine. The evening hunt should be a slam dunk. But once again, the weather had thrown us a wicked curve ball. Usually by mid-September, when the Kansas muzzleloader season opens, lush green vegetation is at a premium. Find it and you find the deer. But the area we were hunting near Abilene, Kansas was as green in September as it usually is in April. Three weeks of late summer rains

The best drives are captained by the hunter who is most familiar with the land and how the deer use it.

had seen to that. With everything green and lush, the deer simply did not have to move far to find their vittles. That makes for poor stand hunting. We were seeing a few deer each evening and morning on

stand, but not the deer Rick had hoped we would see. So Rick, a long, lean bundle of energy who humps a 40-pound mail bag thirteen miles a day in his job as mail carrier, decided that our best option was to get in there after them and see if we could not shake them loose.

The habitat here is ideally suited to deer drives: lots of relatively narrow corridors of timber either in the form of ditches, creek

A nice buck taken by a well-positioned stander during a well-orchestrated drive.

bottoms or tree lines. And yet, on many drives, we never saw a deer. We knew of course that some of the deer were simply holding tight and slipping out the backside after the drivers had passed by. But in the heavy cover the drivers rarely saw them. Yet the drives were our best option. So even with the sun beating down unmercifully and the temperature in the low 90s, we continued to push. Like I said, many of our drives produced nothing, but then there would be a sudden flurry of activity as a buck rammed through heavy cover ahead of the drivers. Both Bryce and Ernie had taken fine eight-point bucks at close range as the bucks tore past their positions at full speed.

Both by the way, were shooting the new Thompson/Center Encore in the Katahdin carbine version. With it's stubby 20-inch ported barrel and halo peep sight, this is a super fast-handling, lightweight muzzleloader that allowed both hunters to get on the fast-moving bucks quickly and accurately. If you happen to be in the market for a muzzleloader and do a lot of hunting in heavy cover, or if weight is a consideration, give the Katahdin Carbine a serious look. The Katahdin Carbine is a real shooter in a lightweight, fast-handling configuration.

On the last day of our hunt heavy rain fell on Kansas. The rain would not have stopped us from hunting, but the lightening did. We waited it out and did not get started until noon. Ernie, who had missed a giant buck on a drive the day before, redeemed himself with a fine shot on a full-bore eight-pointer on our first drive of the day. On a later drive a pair of bucks came past me, but neither was the caliber of buck I was looking to hang my Kansas tag on. I tend to get real fussy in Kansas, because I know what the potential is there. Of all of the states I hunt, I would rate Kansas as being in the top three when it comes to having a realistic opportunity of taking a buck in that 150 and up class. The Kansas deer herd is managed quite well and it shows. But the main reason why I rate Kansas right up there with Iowa and western Illinois and a notch above western Wisconsin, southeast Ohio and up-and-coming Kentucky, is that the deer in Kansas are more visible.

There simply is not the amount of cover in Kansas that there is in the other states mentioned. This means that even though there are probably not more mature deer in Kansas than in any of those other states, you have a better chance of seeing one in Kansas. Actually, this was not the first time I had participated in deer drives during the Kansas September muzzleloader season. About five years ago, I drew a tag for Unit 18 down in the southwest corner of the state and hunted with my friend Jeff Louderback on his family's ranch.

On that hunt, because the weather had been hot and dry for weeks before my arrival, the deer were keying on irrigated alfalfa fields and I was seeing a minimum

In many states, early season whitetail hunts will be limited to bow or muzzleloader. This in-line is a practical choice for muzzleloader-only hunts.

of six bucks each evening. In the mornings I would slip further back into the river bottoms hoping to catch deer coming off the fields and making their way to bed. This tactic had proved successful in terms of seeing deer, I just was not seeing the right buck. Then one morning on stand I saw a real monster. He never got close enough for me to try a shot, but I watched where he headed and felt certain that I knew where the buck had bedded for the day. Slipping out of there took some doing, because a pair of bucks, both of them very respectable, had bedded down about 60 yards from where I

crouched behind a massive cottonwood deadfall. But by using the dry riverbed for cover, I managed to get out of there without spooking the bucks. When I got back to the ranch and told Jeff about what happened he got on the phone to his Dad. It so happened that his Dad and his uncle were just saddling up thier horses to go round up cattle in the river bottom. While Jeff saddled up his horse, Cowboy, to go help his uncle and Dad, I hustled back to the riverbottom, crawled my way up the dry river bed and got in position.

That cattle drive/deer drive was one of the more unusual deer hunts I have ever

If drivers move slowly, the deer will move slowly ahead of them and provide standers with good shots at standing or walking targets.

participated in. I could hear the drive long before I could see it. Those cows did not want to be disturbed and they were voicing their displeasure. But I can now tell you from personal experience that a hundred head of beef being moved through the timber by three cowboys makes for a very effective deer drive. Several does and fawns and a couple of small bucks had already passed within easy range of my position when the cattle drive reached the chunk of timber where I suspected Mr. Big was bedded. I expected him to break and run towards me at any moment, but the cattle got closer and closer and the big buck did not show himself. A fine eight-pointer did, but I let him go. And then, with the lead cows in sight, I saw that big buck casually slip out behind the cattle drive and cross that dry river bed. Like I said, the big ones are real cool customers.

The story had a happy ending though. The two bucks that had bedded down so close to me that morning got up and came across in front of me. It was a tough decision knowing which one to take. One was a big eight-point, the other a non-typical with a very narrow, but heavy rack. They

Both the standers and the drivers take pride in a successful drive.

were on the move and there was not much time to decide. I settled on the non-typical, swung with him as he scooted across the dry river bed, over led him just a tad and broke his neck as he scrambled up the far bank. I was pleased with that fine buck, but I was even more impressed with the display of nerves that big buck had displayed in the face of a deer drive featuring 100 Herefords, three horses and a trio of whooping cowboys. But this time there

Drivers should move slowly, especially through the heaviest cover.

were no cows, no horses and no cowboys. Just Ernie, Bryce and Rick doing their best to try to move a buck or two towards where J. Wayne, Ken and I waited.

On one of our last drives of the day, I was positioned at one corner of a 120-acre patch of cover which consisted mainly of scattered wild plum thickets. Some of these thickets were no bigger than your garage, while others were the size of a football field. Surrounding the thickets was knee-high grass and low-growing buck brush. Because my vantage point was located on a high knob I had a commanding view of the entire 120 acres.

As Rick, Ernie and Bryce entered the far corner of the cover, Ernie and Bryce went around one side of a large plum thicket while Rick, who I am convinced is part beagle, plowed right through the middle of it. A small fork-horn broke out behind Rick and ran all the way to where I stood before disappearing into another plum thicket not 20 yards from my position. Then another buck broke. This one too came out behind Rick. Through my 10x42 glasses I could see that he was a mature buck carrying an impressive eight-point rack. If he followed the same course the fork-horn had taken, he was going to be in trouble. But big bucks are often cool customers and this was one of them.

He stood his ground until he had Rick's position pinpointed and then simply slipped

Ernie French took a fall and nearly landed a ten-point buck shortly after I snapped this photo.

back around the backside of the plum thicket and disappeared. All I could do was tip my hat in admiration. As the drivers closed in on our positions, Ernie took a nasty fall while busting through one of the plum thickets. I could hear Ernie crashing in the brittle limbs. Then I heard more crashing and Ernie hollered "Holy Cow!" Ernie had nearly landed on a ten-point buck. Odds are good that if Ernie had not stumbled and fallen, the buck would have held tight and let Ernie pass within just a few yards of where he lay. When the buck broke cover, he stopped momentarily in the open where both Ken and I had a clear shot at him, but since we knew that Ernie was somewhere in the thicket right behind the buck, neither of us took the shot. In less time than it takes for me to type this sentence, the ten-pointer pinpointed the location of all three drivers and then scooted right back through them.

With the drive over, Rick and Ernie were discussing the buck that had just escaped, when another big buck, this one a dandy with stickers jutting off of long points, jumped up a few yards away and followed the ten-pointer back into the heart of that 120-acre plumb thicket. And that my friends is how big bucks get big.

Standers should take up positions where they can use a tree for both cover and a rifle rest.

Chapter Eleven

The POST-RUT BLUES

I n my experience, there is not a tougher time of the season to take a good buck than during the two- to three-week period following the end of breeding, a time we hunters call the post-rut. During this period, everything is working against you and nothing is in your favor. With that said, I can tell you that each year I spend a lot of time hunting during post-rut conditions. Like you, if it comes down to hunting the post-rut or not hunting at all, I'll hunt the post-rut every time. Part of the reason I spend so much time hunting during post-rut is that many of the best states for big whitetail deer hold their firearms seasons during the post-rut. In fact, that is one of the big reasons why states like Iowa, Kansas, Wisconsin and Illinois lead the parade when it comes to putting big bucks in the books. All of these states hold their general firearm season after the rut is over, when all bucks of breeder age are the least vulnerable. A buck of

The post-rut is a tough time to hunt, but I've taken some nice bucks like this tall-tined Iowa 150-class buck, during the post-rut period.

Don't kid yourself; the post-rut is a tough time to hunt for a good buck. Figure on paying your dues.

breeding age gives it all he's got during the rut. As we have seen, it actually begins during pre-rut, the rubbing, the scrape making, checking and freshening scrapes, sorting things out with rival bucks, constantly checking on the status of each doe he can find. Heck, by the time the first doe actually comes into heat, a buck has already expended a lot of effort in this business we call rutting. And then he really gets down to business.

For the next three weeks the buck spends all of his time either searching for a hot doe, tending a hot doe, protecting that doe from other bucks, or breeding that doe. There is precious little time to eat, even less time to rest. And so when the rut is over, and the last available doe has been bred, all that buck wants to do is find a quiet place, bed down and recuperate. He will eat and drink, but mostly this will be at night. For now he needs rest.

In a couple of weeks, when the weather turns colder and winter is in the air, that will change, but for now, rest, not food, is high priority. For now, he is content to just lay in that cedar swamp, or in that nasty tangle of blowdowns or maybe just over the crest of that ridge, where he can see anything approaching from below and will be able to smell anything coming over the other side of the ridge.

How do you hunt a deer with no reason to move? There are four options that work best for post-rut bucks. Which you choose to use should be based primarily upon weather conditions, hunting pressure and your personal skill level. The four options are still-hunting, which is the most difficult of the four and has the lowest success rate, stand hunting in heavy cover where you suspect the buck is bedding, small drives, or letting other hunters move the deer past your location. Most mature bucks that are taken during the post-rut are taken by hunters employing option number four, but let's look at each in the order I listed them.

STILL-HUNTING FOR POST-RUT BUCKS

I've taken seven bucks by still-hunting during the post-rut and even though you might not consider them all trophies merely by sizing up their racks, I can tell you that I regard each of those seven bucks as a trophy in the very truest sense of the word. I took them by skill, not luck. Now don't get me wrong, I've got nothing against being lucky. Like you, I've hung my tag on some deer that could be racked up to luck, not skill. But when it comes to still-hunting, luck is not much of a factor. This is my favorite way to hunt and yet I rarely have the opportunity. The reason is that only a few times each season are conditions ripe for still-hunting.

For the still-hunter to have any chance of success, he must be able to move quietly through the woods. This means that the forest duff has to be wet from rain, snow or perhaps dew or melting frost. There are

*If you are still-hunting during the post-rut, use binoculars
to carefully check out possible buck cover.*

those who attempt to hunt on foot when the leaves underfoot are like Rice Krispies. They will tell you that they are still-hunting, but they are not. They are just walking around the woods hoping to get lucky and jump up a deer within range. Even when conditions are perfect, the deer have the edge over the still-hunters. It is a lot easier for a deer to see, hear or smell you before you are able to spot the deer. If you are new to still-hunting, just accept that fact. White flags waving good-bye are part of the game when you still-hunt. But if you are patient enough to calculate each step you take, if you spend more time stationary then you do moving, if you use binoculars to pick cover apart before you advance, and if you wear quiet outer clothing of fleece or wool and soft-soled boots which allow you to feel that stick underfoot before it cracks, then maybe, just maybe one day you will know what it is like to sneak within range of a post-rut buck. It's a good feeling.

TAKE A STAND IN HEAVY COVER

This one will test the patience of the most patient hunter. The idea here is that a buck is going to bed down in heavy cover where he is least likely to be disturbed. If you know, or think you know, which patch of cover that is, then you have a chance of taking that buck when he arrives at this location at first light in the morning, when he stirs from his bed at mid-day to stretch, relieve himself and

perhaps browse for a bit, and again at dusk, when he will rise from his day bed to feed for the evening. But I will warn you now that I have known only a few hunters who have the mental stamina to pull an all day sit on a stand in heavy cover waiting and hoping for that one chance. Trying to hunt these locations for only the morning or evening hunt will generally ruin them because the buck will detect you as you depart the morning stand or when you attempt to access your stand for the evening hunt. These stands are not set on the edge of bedding cover, but right in the bedroom itself.

If you are only going to hunt mornings and evenings, then a stand along the edge is a better bet. Here you are trying to catch the buck as he slips into his bedding area in that pink light of dawn, or hoping to catch him slipping out in the evening. Of the two, morning is by far the best bet. During the post-rut, most big bucks simply do not depart the heavy cover until dark. They may stir within the cover at dusk, but by the time they actually exit the cover it is often too dark to shoot. But in the morning, I have found that many bucks arrive at their sanctuaries during that first half hour of daylight just prior to sunrise.

It was my second day in the stand and I was going nuts. The day before I had climbed into the stand well before first light and had not climbed down until dark. It is tough to go back to a stand

If the weather turns nasty during the post-rut, count yourself lucky, because the deer will be forced to move more to search for the best available food sources.

from which you have not seen a deer. It is doubly difficult to go back to a stand from which you not only have not seen a deer, but just can't see period! But I was convinced that my best chance of scoring on a mature buck on the midwestern farm I was hunting was to haunt the best cover on the farm. That cover just happened to be in the shape of 30-some acres of spruce and pine which the landowner had planted nearly 20 years ago.

The trees had not been planted for timber, just for wildlife habitat and erosion control, so they were planted close together and never thinned. Now they stood 20 feet high and shoulder to shoulder, forming an almost unbroken sea of dark green. Just the kind of place a big buck likes to hang out.

I had found enough rubs and old scrapes along the perimeter of the stand of conifers to justify my hunch that the evergreens served as the daytime refuge of a good buck. Now it was late afternoon on the second day. With nearly 20 hours of staring at the same green walls surrounding me, I was finding it hard to concentrate and finding it even more difficult to keep up my optimism for my stand.

Maybe I should have hunted the perimeter of the stand of evergreens, or maybe the oak ridge would have been a better choice, surely I would have at least seen some deer at either place. By the sound of the gun shots I had heard the last two days, other hunters were finding plenty of action in the more open timber. But then

I reminded myself that I was not out here to see a bunch of deer. I had come for one very special buck and everything I knew about mature deer pointed toward this conifer thicket as the most likely place to make his acquaintance.

I heard a stick crack somewhere off to my left. I shifted the rifle into position and strained to hear another sound while trying to look through that solid wall of green, but I never did hear another sound. Like their kind so often do, the buck just materialized. At first I saw only the tips of his antlers, then his head and neck and finally his chest. The rifle bucked and the deer went down. He lay only fifteen steps from the base of the tree in which I sat. I could have shot twice that far to the front of my stand, not much further to the right. Few hunters will sit such claustrophobic stands sites, which is exactly why these tight places are so good for big bucks. Many of the encounters I have had with big bucks in claustrophopic cover have taken place while I was hunting other game.

As a kid, my buddies and I would often hunt cottontail rabbits over a loud-mouthed beagle named Tinker Bell. There were not a lot of deer around the area where we lived back then, but it seemed that every big buck we ever saw was rousted out of some God-forsaken bramble patch that even the rabbits had trouble getting through.

Then while hunting pheasants behind my father's half-broke Labrador (a dog he never could break from running deer), it was not unusual for a fat-assed, corn-fattened, heavy-horned, farm-country buck

The post rut is a good time to still-hunt slowly through places where you suspect deer to be holding.

to come blasting out of some impossible tangle of willow and slough grass with that black demon hard on his hooves. Pa would scream at the dog until he was blue in the face and then we would just sit down and wait for the dog to come back (which usually took about fifteen minutes). Luckily there were not nearly as many deer around then as there are now or we would have spent all day waiting for that dog.

Even while duck hunting I was getting lessons in the places big bucks go to be left alone. Many times on opening day of the deer season, Pa and I would be sitting over a spread of mallard decoys in a big cattail marsh and have a deer or two swim through our decoys. All of them were big bucks. I didn't know it then, but I know now that those bucks were not just crossing that big cattail marsh to get to another patch of timber. They were looking for a half-dry hummock in the marsh where they could hide out for the day. Most of those bucks probably died of old age.

Those early experiences were the foundation for my penchant today for hunting big bucks in tight cover. Wherever I travel to hunt the whitetail the first thing I look for on the land I will be hunting is the nastiest cover available. I suppose that somewhere there might be cover so thick, so thorn-laden, so muddy, so impenetrable that a whitetail refuses to enter it, but if such cover exists I've never found it.

This of course is not news to most whitetail hunters. Many of you hunt the

I've taken some of my best post-rut bucks while hunting during some tough weather conditions.

edges of thick cover. Many more hunt the trails, the saddles and the funnels deer will hopefully use as they travel to and from the heaviest cover. But few ever hunt in the thick of it. I don't blame you. It's not fun hunting a place where you can spit about as far as you can shoot. It's nerve wracking to know that there is a deer within just a few yards of you, to be able to hear the sucking sound his hooves make as he pulls them from the mud with each step he takes and not be able to see a single hair.

Many times after a fruitless day or two in some hell-hole I've sworn never again. But of course I never keep my word. It's too late

In northern states, there is often snow on the ground during the post-rut period. Snow can be a huge help in determining where deer are moving.

for me, I've seen too much, too many big bruisers twisting and turning their racks as they somehow maneuver through a wall of bramble, briar and vines. After all of this time, all of the deer, I suppose I should no longer be amazed, but I am.

I only know of one way to hunt these places. You get there early, long before the first glimpse of day and you claw your way into your stand. Usually the higher the stand the better because the more holes and pockets you can look down into from your perch, the better the odds that you might just get a glimpse of him. However there are circumstances when a stand lower in a tree or even a ground blind will actually provide better visibility than a stand high in a tree. The most common of these circumstances is when hunting in conifers. Spruce, fir and younger pines all have heavy, thick branches which droop nearly to the ground. From above, it is sometimes impossible to see down through this canopy of branches, but from ground level you can look beneath the branches where deer travel. Bring along plenty of grub, some water, and if it's cold, an extra layer or two because to hunt these places right you are going to be there until dark or until you put him on the ground, whichever comes first. If you give up during the day and climb down, you can forget about hunting that stand again the next day. In this cover you can't make a quiet exit and he will know you have been there. Once he knows, he may continue to use the cover, but he won't go near where he heard

you, you can bet on that. Your best chance will come in the first half hour of shooting light. Big bucks don't hang around the fields and open timber until it is full light like other deer sometimes do. In fact, by the time younger deer have decided it is time to vacate the places where they have fed for the night, big deer are already in their security cover. Only during the rut will you sometimes catch a big bruiser slinking his way back home in the full light of morning after a long night of carousing with the boys and chasing the lady deer. But now, in the post-rut, the big ones almost always are tucked away for the day before full light. I've been hunting the thick stuff for a long time now and I still don't like it. Never having done hard time I don't know what it feels like when that whistle blows and you are ushered back into your cell, but I suspect it is something like climbing into a stand in the nasty stuff for that third or fourth day in row. Nope, there's nothing aesthetically pleasing about these places, but when the guns start going off on the ridges and down in the valleys, I don't know of a better place to be waiting on Mr. Big.

DRIVES

My personal preference when it comes to deer hunting leans heavily towards stand hunting and when conditions are ideal, still-hunting. But there are times when a deer drive is the best tactic for producing some action. When deer are not moving naturally, which is normally the case during the post-rut, or when there are not enough hunters in the woods to keep them on the move, a well organized deer drive is a good option. This may be an oversimplification, but it seems to me that deer drives can be divided into two categories: big drives and small drives.

Big drives employ a large number of hunters and small drives only a few hunters. Big drives take in a good chunk of territory with each sweep, small drives a much smaller parcel of whitetail habitat. Personally, I have never participated in a big drive which was not both confusing and counter-productive. How can a drive be counter-productive you might ask? Well, when all of the deer in the area to be driven either slip out the sides, circle back behind the drivers or simply hold their ground and let the drivers walk on past, all you have accomplished is to render that chunk of ground now unsuitable for either stand hunting or still-hunting. That, in my book, is counter-productive.

Small drives are sometimes not much better. The only difference is that when a small drive turns into a mess, at least it only ruins a small parcel of ground for stand hunting or still-hunting. I don't waste my time participating in big drives anymore. If there are more than six hunters involved, you can count me out. The most effective drives with which I have been involved were conducted by only three or four hunters and sometimes just a pair of hunters. In fact, my favorite drive really is

Well-overestimated deer drives are often the only way to get bucks up and moving during tough post-rut conditions.

probably not a drive at all. Instead, it is just one hunter slowly still-hunting towards another hunter or perhaps two hunters who are patiently sitting on stand.

Sometimes, while the "drive" is underway, one of the hunters will shoot a deer that wandered past the stand on its own and not because of the drive. Just as often, the still-hunter/driver will slip up on a deer and kill it. It is important to put your most patient hunters on stand and your stealthiest to the task of still-hunting. The idea here is not to spook deer, but no matter how good a hunter is at still-hunting some deer are going to see, hear or smell him and slip away from him. The hope is that if the standers are in good locations one of those deer will slip by within range. It works often enough to be worth a try when deer movement is non-existent.

My hunting partner and brother-in-law Larry Boughten and I sometimes do a two-man drive in which we basically pick out an area and then still-hunt slowly towards each other. I call it playing "hopscotch." Larry moves on the hour and sits on the half hour, I do the opposite coming from the other direction. We try to do it in places where both of us are hunting with a crosswind. It takes a couple of hours to "drive" a small valley or ridgeline this way, but the best drives are slow moving affairs. Drives like this produce high percentage shots at walking or stationary deer. Big, noisy drives designed to startle deer usually result in hunters flinging a lot of useless led at running deer.

Another two-man drive that works is to have one hunter take a stand and then have another hunter slowly still-hunt in a big circle around the hunter on stand. This one works because deer do not often simply follow a straight line when evading hunters. When a deer sneaks away from the hunter walking the big circle, it might show itself to the hunter on the stand. Standers often choose to take up a position where they can cover a wide open field or other open area, but this is usually a mistake. Most deer won't cross that opening and if they do, they will do so in high gear. You are better off taking a stand inside the timber.

Most drives are doomed before they ever get started for one of two reasons. Either the standers spook the deer while getting to their stands or the drivers begin the drive before the standers are in position. The way to solve this problem is to give the standers twice as much time as you think is needed to get in position. This way the standers will not feel rushed and will sneak into their stands, lessening the risk of spooking deer in the process.

I'll warn you now that mature deer are cool customers when it comes to deer drives. They have played this game before. They know when to sneak, when to run and when to hold tight. And they have nerves of titanium. The best example of just how reluctant a mature buck can be to vacate his best cover took place many years ago. But time has not diminished the importance of the lesson I learned on that day.

Back when I was just out of high school a group of buddies and I saw a big buck and a doe enter a football shaped patch of scrub willow and slough grass that was completely surrounded by plowed field. With spirits high, we positioned standers and then commenced to line up and push that five-acre hell-hole. A doe broke on the first push. On the second I killed a nice eight-pointer as he exploded from cover nearly at my feet. On the fourth push the big buck got up just before P.T.

would have stepped on him, but tangled in vines, P.T. could not get a shot and the big buck slipped back behind the drivers. On the seventh push through the slough the big buck pulled the same stunt when another member of the group nearly stepped on him. After ten pushes and several hours, sweating, muddy to our hips, exhausted and befuddled, we quit and went looking elsewhere. I doubt we could have forced that buck out of that thicket with twice as many drivers.

Like I said, I'm not real big on deer drives, but there are times when a deer drive is the very best option for getting a crack at a post-rut buck.

Major bucks know the places they can go to escape hunting pressure.
They return to these same places season after season.

RELY UPON HUNTING PRESSURE

When the firearms deer season opens, the single most important factor dictating success will not be how well-traveled the trail in front of your stand might be, how big the scrapes are, the size or number of rubs, how thick the bedding area is, or how plentiful the food supply. Under normal conditions, all of these "signs" would be of importance, but there is nothing normal about opening weekend. Unless you are fortunate enough to hunt your own property, there are few places in the country where hunting pressure will not be the main catalyst for deer movement on the opening weekend of the season.

There is a very simple rule I try to adhere to anytime hunting pressure is a factor in deer movement. One, I determine where the pressure will originate (Point A) and two, determine where the deer will be headed for once the guns start barking (Point B). If you know of a Point A and a Point B in the area you hunt, you are in business. If you do not, get yourself an aerial photograph of the area you hunt. With an aerial photograph it is easy to pick out all of the potential Point As and Point Bs in your hunting area. In fact, even if you have hunted the same area for years, you will find an aerial photograph to be an invaluable tool.

Once you have this information, your next decision is whether you position yourself between Point A and Point B, or take a stand within the escape cover itself, which is Point B. I let my familiarity with the land or an aerial photograph help with this decision. If there is a natural or man-made funnel somewhere along the route the deer will be most likely to take as they move from the source of the most intense hunting pressure to the sanctuary of escape cover, my stand will overlook this pinch-point.

Common funnels are a narrow strip of high ground between lakes or sloughs, a fence line connecting two woodlots, that place where the woods along the creek narrows to only 100 yards. You get the idea. Anyplace where lateral deer movement is restricted is a funnel and there is not a better place you can be sitting on opening morning.

If you cannot find a funnel, you are probably better off setting up on the edge of the escape cover or within the escape cover itself. Most of the time the escape cover will be the thickest, nastiest cover in the area. Look for the kind of stuff hunters walk around instead of through. If it is wet, so much the better. Old deer have found refuge in these places before. The old deer introduce the young deer to these places. Consequently, good escape cover is used by deer year after year. The deer simply crawl into these hell-holes and stay put until dark.

I'll warn you now that hunting these places is not much fun. If the place is worth hunting you won't be able to see very far. With shots ringing out all around you, staying put on a stand in one of these thick places becomes a real mind game. My brain is always screaming at me to abandon ship and get out there in the open woods where I can see something. And I'll admit that I have spent all day on stand in these nasty places and not seen a single deer. But more often than not, hunting the places other hunters do not pays dividends.

Besides being in the right place, you need to be there at the right time. Since I have no way of knowing if a buck is going to show at dawn, high noon or just before the end of shooting hours, I just hunt all day. Lots of hunters claim to hunt all day, but few actually do. Most climb down from their stands or get up from their seat against the stump to go for a little walk to warm up, to check on their buddies, to meet for lunch, to help Joe drag out his buck, or maybe to put on a drive or two with friends. All of that activity is what keeps deer on the move and anytime deer are on the move the best place to be is on stand overlooking a high travel area. Sounds simple, but it is not. Staying put all day on stand, no matter how good the stand, is tough. That is why so few hunters can pull it off and why those who do rarely fail to use their tag.

For nearly 50 years my wife Nancy's family has hunted the same valley in the Whitewater WMA near our home in southeast Minnesota. For most of the

You hear and read a lot about hunting in funnels, and with good reason. As Pat Reeve knows, shown here with a fine Wisconsin buck, funnels are ultra-dependable stand locations.

past 30 years I have joined them. When there were a lot of youngsters coming along, our group often numbered a dozen or more. These days we are down to three or four. We have drug a lot of venison up those steep hills. Over half of the deer taken during the past 30 years have been taken by only two hunters in that group. Why? Because they are both good sitters; into the stand before first light and down when shooting hours are over. Some call it boring. I call it deadly.

Chapter Twelve

⚜

CORN STALKS

Each December, when the snow falls hard and the winter winds push down out of Canada, I get an itch to hunt the corn. I've got a guy named Toad Smith to blame for that. Toad was a bearded, gentle giant of a man who hailed from Iowa. He got me started stalking the corn for deer even though we never actually got a chance to hunt together. Toad died of a massive heart attack before we could complete that mission. But on an ice fishing trip the winter before Toad died, Toad and I spent a lot of time between bites (and in ice fishing, there can be a lot of time between bites sometimes), talking about deer hunting. Toad told me how he loved to stalk standing corn for deer during the late season and he told me just how to go about it. So the next winter, I did and it was just like Toad had said, "There just ain't nuthin' quite like sneakin' up on a deer in the corn. Once you try it and sneak on that first deer, you'll be hooked for life." So come on

Binoculars are invaluable when stalking in corn to positively identifying suspicious objects like rocks, weeds and dirt clumps that can look a lot like a piece of deer to the naked eye.

There is nothing more thrilling in the world of whitetail hunting than slipping up to within a couple of yards of a buck like this in standing corn.

along, and I'll share with you what Toad taught me. But first, let me tell you about my first hunt in the corn.

A few days after Christmas, a blizzard blew in out of Canada and raged across southeast Minnesota, where I live. That storm left a foot of new snow, a biting northwest wind and sub-zero temperatures in it's wake. The fall had been wet, hampering the harvest and there were still a few unharvested cornfields. I had

permission to hunt one 80-acre field a few miles from my home. I parked the pickup along the side of the just plowed road at mid-morning, pulled on whites and started crisscrossing the field. On my second pass I spotted a deer bedded down about 50 yards away. My binoculars showed it to be a small buck. It would not have mattered, a doe would have been just as exciting. I backed up a dozen rows and began to sneak in the direction of the buck, counting my steps as I went. When I got to 35 steps, I began to slip cross-row once again, moving only when the steady northwest wind gusted enough to obliterate any sounds I made. When I caught a glimpse of dark hide between stalks, I estimated the buck to be no more than ten yards away, but there was no way to get an arrow to the target. I crept closer. Blood pounded in my temples and despite the cold I felt uncomfortably warm. The old adrenalin was really pumping. Inch by cautious inch I closed the distance, looking for an opening to the bucks vitals.

When only three rows (that's under three yards!) separated us, I saw my opening, a six inch gap, which, if I had the buck's posture interpreted correctly, would put the broadhead neatly through both of his lungs. In the instant before the shot, the wind died momentarily and I realized that I could hear the buck chewing his cud. That's getting up close and personal! I drew and released in one motion. The buck exploded from his bed, ran 50 yards and died in mid-stride. Toad had been right in his warning. I was hooked on stalking deer in standing corn. Each year as fall gives way to winter I pray for the right weather for stalking the corn.

THE RIGHT WEATHER

Specific conditions are required for successful cornfield hunting. You need standing corn, but not too much standing corn. Over much of the best whitetail habitat, especially in the Midwest, corn is the number one agricultural crop. Deer use the corn for both food and cover from about mid-July right up until the corn is harvested. Looking for deer in standing corn when there are thousands of acres of standing corn available to them is a waste of time. I don't even consider hunting the corn until at least 75 percent of the corn crop has been harvested. Deer that have become accustomed to living in standing corn will move from one field to another as the corn is harvested.

What you are looking for is a situation where deer are forced to concentrate in a limited number of fields. In my early days of stalking the corn I hunted only cornfields which were adjacent to woods or a short distance from timber. Because we tend to associate whitetail deer with woodlands it is difficult to imagine them living in an environment where the nearest timber might be a mile or two away. But deer have no qualms about using a cornfield which is a long hike away from any woods. In fact, since hunting the standing corn has caught on with other bowhunters, I often look for these isolated fields. Rarely does anyone else bother to hunt them.

Once you have found a field you must obtain permission from the landowner to hunt the field. At first some landowners have been reluctant to allow me to tromp in their cornfields, but when I explain the method I use to hunt and insure them that I will not damage their crop nearly as much as the critters I am hunting, most of them just shake their heads in sympathy at this poor fool who thinks he can walk into a cornfield with a stick and string and come out dragging a deer. Since most landowners are aware of the damage deer can do to a corn crop, they are more than happy to have me reduce the problem.

Then you need wind; the more wind the better. Wind rustles cornstalks and that rustling is what allows you to stalk through the corn without being picked up by the whitetail's acute sense of hearing. Without wind deer will hear you coming long before you ever get close enough to see them. In my experience, the wind needs to be blowing at least ten mph for stalking the corn to be effective. 15 or 20 mph is better. The biggest mistake most hunters make is attempting to hunt standing corn when there is not enough wind. Hunt when the breeze is not sufficient to cover the sound of your approach and all you do is possibly ruin the field for future hunts. In a pinch you can hunt when the stalks and leaves are sopping wet from rain, wet snow or melted frost, but wind is best.

Snow really helps. I have taken deer in the corn when there is not snow on the ground, so it is not impossible, but deer are much easier to spot when there is snow on the ground. And with snow on the ground you can quickly tell by the tracks and beds you find if the field is worth hunting. If you must hunt when there is not snow, look extra close and scan every row with binoculars. Even then you are going to blunder into some deer that you would not have if there had been snow on the ground.

You can hunt the corn at any time of the day, but the best time to hunt is from mid-morning until mid-afternoon. Most of the deer will be bedded at this time, although deer will frequently get up out of their beds for a short stint around noon. Bedded deer are easier to stalk than deer that are up and feeding. Whitetail deer that have been hunted hard never totally relax, but a deer bedded down in the corn comes as close to relaxed as a whitetail gets. It is interesting to me that while a whitetail in timber is usually a little more nervous than normal on a windy day, most likely because the deer knows that it's senses are compromised by the wind, a deer in the corn is not. I think it is because deer are accustomed to danger in the timber, but have learned that the corn provides a safe sanctuary where they are rarely disturbed.

CLOTHING AND GEAR
FOR STALKING THE CORN

There are camouflage patterns that will make you all but invisible in cornfields, but you don't need special camo to hunt the corn. Patterns with a lot of tan and light brown are great when there is not snow on the ground. And don't forget a

Be sure to wear a full face mask when hunting standing corn. Deer instantly recognize the human face and will spook from it.

Binoculars come in handy for determining if the object you are looking at is the rear end of a deer, a rock, dirt clod or clump of weeds. Don't laugh. By not following my own advice I once pulled off a masterpiece of a stalk on a brown rock complete with a set of milkweed "antlers." Binoculars also help in determining the deer's body position so that you know where to place the arrow. I also use binoculars to search for other deer before beginning my stalk. Nothing will ruin a stalk quicker than accidently "bumping" a deer you didn't see.

A cornfield might seem like a strange place for a grunt call, but I've used a grunt call with good results on several occasions when hunting the corn. Once, when I had successfully stalked to within just a few yards of a buck, I found that the buck's vitals were blocked by a mat of weeds and wind twisted stalks. Rather than risk trying to punch an arrow through the screen of cover, I drew and then grunted softly. The buck stood up and offered me a good shot.

The author with a buck which he stalked and killed in a standing cornfield when there was no snow on the ground.

facemask. When you stick your head into a row to take a peek, an uncovered mug can easily give you away. When there is snow on the ground I like snow camouflage, all white or gray. Wool, fleece or brushed cotton are all quiet.

I prefer to hunt fields of standing corn where there is snow on the ground, but if you go extra slow, you can successfully hunt standing corn with no snow on the ground.

On other hunts I have used a grunt call to lure in bucks that were on their feet instead of bedded. Sometimes, when a buck is moving around, it is safer to bring him to you than risk a stalk on a moving target.

A rangefinder will sometimes work for taking a reading when you spot a bedded deer, but often there are too many stalks and leaves in the way to get a good reading. If you have one, bring it with you, but don't rush out and buy one just to hunt the corn.

You don't need anything special in the way of archery gear for hunting in the corn, although I think it helps to be able to shoot instinctively. Peep sights and pins can be a handicap when the range is short and the opening tiny. With a little backyard practice anyone can learn to hit what they are looking at by shooting instinctively at targets at short range. A recurve is the ideal bow for the corn, but a compound will do the job. I have a friend who has a couple of special "cornfield arrows" that he uses only when stalking deer in standing corn. His cornfield arrows have a stiffer spine than the arrows he normally shoots and do not have any fletching. My friend claims that feathers or vanes only get in the way when stalking cornfields and are unnecessary for stabilizing arrow flight at the short ranges commonly encountered in the cornfields. As for the stiff spine, my friend claims that shafts with a stiff spine flex less when leaving the bow meaning that there is less chance of the arrow sideswiping a cornstalk and being thrown off target. My friend takes a lot of deer in standing corn, so I don't argue with him.

HOW TO HUNT STANDING CORN

Ideally the wind should be blowing with the rows, not across them. If the wind is blowing across the rows, odds are good that some of the deer in the field will get your scent and sneak off before you ever see them. You can lessen the odds of deer smelling you by taking extra precautions with odor control. I never hunt the corn without wearing one and often two layers of Scent-Lok clothing.

Start at the downwind end of the field and move slowly across the field one row at a time. Never step foot into a row until you have looked down that row and determined that there are no deer in the row. I like to hold my bow against my chest so that it does not hang up on cornstalks.

Once you reach the far end of the field walk upwind as far as you could see down the rows, usually 40 to 60 yards, cut into the corn and start across one row at a time. Keep doing this until you either finish the field or spot a deer. When you spot a deer you can take the shot if the deer is close enough, but most of the time you will need to stalk the deer. This is where cornfield hunting really gets exciting.

Calm down enough to estimate the distance to the deer or take a reading with your rangefinder. Take a good look at the deer through your binoculars and determine which way it is facing. This information is invaluable since once you are in position to shoot you may not be able to see the entire deer. And don't forget to take a look around for other deer. Does and fawns especially are rarely alone. Now move back about 15 rows and slowly sneak in the direction of the deer while counting your steps. Take your time on the final approach. The deer is not going anywhere. Rush it now and you might blow the whole thing.

Sometimes you can slip into the row the deer is bedded in for the shot and other times you will need to shoot cross-row. Each situation is different, so take the time to analyze the circumstances. There is no need to be in a hurry. If the wind is blowing hard enough for you to have gotten that close, odds are good it will not swirl and betray you, so take your time and make the right decisions. Stalking deer in standing corn is pure excitement. I'm so hooked on it that each winter after the deer season is closed I go out and stalk deer in the corn just for fun. Several times I have been able to stalk close enough to bedded deer in the corn that I could reach out and touch them. Toad was right.

Bucks that spend a lot of time in the cornfields grow hog fat.

Chapter Thirteen

⸎

The BITTER END

When I started hunting whitetail deer there were very few opportunities for late-season hunting. But as whitetail deer increased in numbers state game agencies began using late season hunts, primarily with muzzleloader and archery, as tools for helping to control the burgeoning herds while at the same time providing many hours of enjoyment for those of us who are too stubborn or maybe just to darn dumb to hang it before the bitter end. During the past 20 years late-season opportunities for hunting whitetail deer have become increasingly common. I now log 30 to 40 days of deer hunting in December and January each year, months that used to be good only for sitting around the fire and reliving November hunts. There have been hundreds of articles written about late-season deer hunting. Most of them follow a common theme, namely, find the food and you will find the deer. While I'll admit that finding a food source is

I took this stout eight-point buck on a December muzzleloader hunt in Nebraska. Nebraska is one of many states that hold a special muzzleloader season late in the year.

There are few thrills in whitetail hunting that match finding a track and staying with it until you find that buck in your sights. The "bitter end" often provides the best tracking opportunities of the year.

time my out-of-state hunts for when the weather provided what I considered to be optimum conditions (namely deep snow and brutal cold). After all, everything I thought I knew and everything I had ever read on late-season whitetail hunting indicated that the deeper the snow and the lower the temperatures, the better the hunting. But I believe I've been wrong.

I'm now convinced that the best late-season opportunities occur after the first winter storm of the season. For years I dismissed these wimpy storms as mere harbingers of better things to come. I wasn't looking for a couple of inches of snow and temps in the single digits. I wanted a rip-roaring blizzard that closed schools and interstate highways. Anything above the zero mark was balmy in my book. Don't get me wrong, I've been fortunate and have taken some nice bucks in some really nasty conditions, but in all of those situations, I now believe I missed the best hunting of the late season.

The first winter storm of the season seems to be a shocker to the deer. They are not yet accustomed to snow and cold and the sudden appearance of both throw them into a feeding frenzy. I've seen fields fill up with deer in the middle of the day in the aftermath of the first cold snap of the winter. But more importantly, that first winter storm encourages the deer to hit the chow line early enough in the evening that you and I can take advantage of their urgency to get to food. As the winter

important, if it were as simple as that, we late-season hunters would only have to freeze our butts off for an hour or two instead of for days. As I see it, food is only one of the pieces of the late-season puzzle.

DON'T WAIT

Because I usually hunt several states during the late-season, I would try to wears on, instead of the deer coming to the food source earlier and earlier each day, they actually arrive later and later.

I believe that there are two main reasons for this phenomenon. One is the shock effect the first blast of winter has on the deer herd. It must be like having your favorite supermarket burn down during the night. You wake up in the morning and wonder where you are going to get your groceries. Deer probably wonder too, when overnight all of the leftover corn, soybeans and acorns get buried under white, wet stuff.

Usually that first blast of winter arrives in early- to mid-December when most deer are trying to stack on a little extra fat for the coming hard months and the big breeder bucks are desperate to replace the fat reserves they ran off while chasing does in November.

Since the deer are already spending the bulk of their time at this time of the year seeking out the best of rapidly dwindling food sources, the sudden onset of winter seems to throw them into a panic. The most predictable activity of the late season occurs during the few days

following the first winter storm of the season.

Here is an interesting fact which biologists have discovered: As the winter weather continues, deer require less food, not more, as most hunters have long assumed. Decreased metabolic activity and a reduction in thyroid functions, probably triggered by photoperiodism, makes it possible for deer to decrease

Many of the best late season whitetail hunting opportunities take place in northern states that hold special muzzleloader seasons late in the year.

their food intake by up to 30 percent during the winter. As their bodies become accustomed to the snow and cold, deer will cut their daily movements in half. To the deer this is simply a way of conserving energy. For us hunters it means that we now have half the chance we had just a few weeks ago.

This concept was vividly and painfully played out for me one recent December. Snow and cold made an early appearance across the northern midwest that year. Winter had a lock on the land well before Christmas. In mid-December when I began hunting a small farm in western Wisconsin, there had already been snow on the ground for a week or more. I knew after just a couple of days that I was in trouble. The only food source on the farm were two alfalfa fields that were now buried under a foot of heavy, wet snow. In other years, deer had dug through the snow to reach the green alfalfa, but not this year. Without a good food source I was really spinning my wheels, but still I stubbornly tried to make something happen by hanging stands and hunting over the two marginal trails that crossed the property. Before I knew it I had wasted a week.

I made a call to my friend Tom and explained my predicament. "No problem," Tom insured me, "I know of a standing bean field which is being hammered every evening. Last night I videoed over 30 deer on the field and there were a half dozen decent bucks. Come on over and I'll show you where it's at."

An hour later I pulled up to Tom's front door and an hour after that I had a stand hung overlooking a deer trail that looked like Big Jake and the cowboys had pushed a herd of longhorns down it. It was cold and snowing when I hung the bow from a branch stub and settled back in the stand to wait for the procession of deer to begin. I don't think I've ever been more confident in a late season stand. Three hours later I trudged back to my truck. I had not seen a single deer.

The next evening I tried a different trail with the same results and the third evening I strapped on snowshoes and hiked further back in the timber for what turned out to be another futile attempt. What had happened? The deer had simply reached that stage where they were not stressed for food, so they were arriving at the field of standing beans well after shooting hours. I had missed my window of opportunity.

The same thing happened to me a few years ago in Iowa. I had a late-season muzzleloader tag in my pocket and was waiting for what I considered to be ideal weather conditions before making the trip to the southern part of the state to hunt. A winter storm blew in just before Christmas. I could have slipped down and hunted for two or three days and still made it home for Christmas Eve, but I convinced myself that things were only going to get better.

Good tracking snow is one of the advantages of hunting to the bitter end.

To make sure my muzzleloader will perform in cold weather, I give it the deep-freeze test prior to the season. Load the gun, place it in the deep-freezer overnight, then take it out and shoot it in the morning.

days. Temperatures plunged to 20 below zero. I was probably the only one in Alamakee County enjoying the weather. I figured I had it made. But three days later I knew that once again I had waited too long to make my move. Deer were not moving to the food sources I had located until well after shooting hours. I hunted hard dark-to-dark for ten straight days and finally killed a dandy buck during the last five minutes of the final day. As I drove back to my Minnesota home I was tickled to death with the buck, but I also knew that once again I had missed the best opportunity of the late season.

That same buck taught me another lesson. I knew where the buck was feeding and I hunted that location each evening that the wind was in my favor. The first three days it was bitter cold, with temperatures in the minus ten degree range. I saw him twice, but always after shooting hours, although it was still plenty light enough to see the crosshairs on my scope. I would watch him until full dark and then slip out of my ground blind and sneak back to my pickup. Then it got even colder and I

On New Years Eve day, with a major winter storm in the forecast, I pointed the pickup south and arrived just ahead of what turned out to be a real doozy. By the time it was over a foot of new snow lay on top of what the earlier storm had left. Many of the country roads were drifted shut for two

Even in those states where snow rarely falls, late season muzzleloader or archery hunts can provide good action on deer which are forced to key on the best of the dwindling food sources available this late in the season.

THE LATE SEASON LAW:
IF IT CAN GO WRONG, IT WILL

You know all of those little things that sometimes go wrong and spoil an opportunity during the fall? Well, during the late season, all of those little things are magnified several times. You can't get away with any miscues during the late season because the deer are super-spooky after having been hunted for three or more months.

I know that you have read a thousand times that you should practice shooting with your winter clothing on, but now you have read it 1001 times. I practice while wearing my Heater Body Suit. Catch a string on your arm or a collar and all of that late-season dedication and persistence is for nothing.

A bow that is dead quiet in October might creak when it's ten below zero. That creak might not spook an October whitetail, but it will a December buck. To make sure my bow will perform under very cold conditions, I put my bow in the deep-freeze overnight and then take it out and shoot it in the morning. If it doesn't squeak then, it won't when that late-season deer is standing below me.

Ditto for a muzzleloader. If you remove all of the oil and keep the gun dry, you should not have any problems. But to make sure, I load my rifle, put it in the deep-freeze overnight and take it out and shoot it in the morning. If the cold is going to cause the rifle to misfire I want to know it before my hunt.

Stands are another problem. I've had stands that were dead quiet in October squeak and groan every time I shifted my weight when it got really cold. Sometimes you can correct the problem with a little powdered graphite or a dab of Vaseline, but I've got a half dozen stands hanging in the garage that have been permanently retired from late season duty because I can't trust them to be quiet.

Speaking of stands, a piece of carpet or a foam mat on the platform will do more than keep your feet warmer, it will make your stand quieter too. And one more thing, when you do take that late-season deer, be extra careful when you field dress it. When you are cold and excited it is easy to make a wrong cut with the knife.

figured that now the buck would have to feed earlier. But he did not. Not only did the big buck not show up during shooting light, but even the other deer that had been hitting the field in late afternoon, failed to make an appearance before last light.

When I listened to the weather report on the radio after my eighth day of hunting, I almost gave up and went home. A warming trend was moving in. Temps were forecast to rise to near the freezing mark over the next two days. I figured that was the end of any chance I had. If the deer were not getting to the field early in cold weather, they darn sure would not be in a hurry once it warmed up. But being stubborn, I stuck it out.

On the last evening, with the temperatures 50 degrees warmer than when I had begun the hunt ten days before, the big buck sauntered into the field with time to spare. Not only did the buck I had been hunting show that evening, but by the time he arrived on the scene there were more than 20 other deer, including six smaller bucks, already scarfing up the leftover soybeans.

The lesson is simply this: When a warm front falls on the heels of a prolonged cold spell, deer take advantage of it by feeding earlier in the evening. I've also had better hunting in the morning and mid-day during warm spells than I have when the weather is brutal. I think that this can be attributed to the fact that the coldest time of the day is usually right before sunrise. When the temperatures are very low, deer conserve energy by remaining bedded during the coldest hours of the day. But when temperatures moderate, deer revert back to their traditional dawn and dusk feeding patterns.

Deer are difficult to hunt in the mornings if they are bedding very near the food source. The problem is that it is virtually impossible to sneak into a stand between the bedding area and the food source if the two are connected or a short distance apart. When I encounter this situation, I reserve these spots for evening hunts so that I don't bugger them up by trying to hunt them in the morning.

Fortunately, because quality chow is in short supply at this time of the year, some deer travel a mile or more to reach the food source. I like to backtrack these deer to find out where they are bedding and then set up a stand somewhere along that route to intercept them in the mornings. Whenever possible, I position the stand on the edge of the bedding cover so that I can catch those deer that sneak in early and also so that I can be in position for the mid-day activity. Deer usually feed for a short time around mid-day. Normally these mid-day snacks do not mean a trip to the main food source, but just some browsing around the bedding area.

During the rest of the year, when food is abundant, the mid-day feeding period is short, usually a half hour or less, but in the winter, on sun-drenched balmy days, I've often watched deer browse for two or three hours before bedding again. These deer won't move far, often only 100 yards or less from their beds, so you have to be sitting in a stand that is located close to them when they get up and start moving.

You will find that not all bedding areas lend themselves to this kind of up-close-and-personal style of hunting, but if the deer are bedded in conifers that are a favorite winter bedding habitat or are down in other thick, wind-reducing cover, you can usually slip into a stand without blowing the deer out of their beds.

If I'm hunting with a muzzleloader and if conditions are right (meaning soft, not crusted snow), I like to still-hunt during this mid-day feeding period. However, if you have a limited amount of property on which to hunt, hunting from a stand will be a better option. No matter how careful you are, still-hunting will almost certainly disturb some deer and you don't want to screw up the evening hunt by blowing deer out of the bedding area by attempting to still-hunt through it.

One last good shot to end the season.

FORGET ABOUT THAT SECOND RUT STUFF

You know and I know that a few does that did not conceive during the first go-around will be coming into another estrous cycle during the late season. And it's also true that some of the female fawns of the year will enter their first estrous cycle during this period. Many hunters and writers have tried to make a big deal out of this so-called "second rut," but it is nothing compared to the November rut. Pin your late season hopes on a surge of late breeding activity and you are setting yourself up for a disappointment.

A better plan, I believe, is to not anticipate encountering any breeding activity during the late season, but to be prepared to take advantage of it if breeding activity is taking place. If there is a hot doe in the neighborhood, you will know it because a single doe in estrous usually draws a pretty good sized crowd of bucks during the late season.

DON'T BE TOO TOUGH

Late season hunters are a tough bunch. You have to be to go out and sit in a

HOW TO STAY WARM IN THE COLDEST WEATHER

There are darn few guarantees in the world of whitetail hunting, but I will guarantee you this: A Heater Body Suit will keep you warm no matter what Ma Nature hurls in your direction. In fact, the suit comes with that very simple guarantee—if you get cold, send it back.

The Heater Body Suit works on the same principle as a mitten. If you work or play in the cold, you know that a mitten will keep your hands warmer than a glove. That's because a mitten traps all four fingers and your hand in a single enclosure. The Heater Body Suit does not require any batteries, no wires, no gimmicks. You simply climb into the well insulated shell, boots and all, zip it up and let the heat generated from your own body keep you toasty warm in the nastiest of conditions.

When you see a deer, you silently unzip the suit and let suit fall off of your shoulders where unique shoulder straps hold the suit out of the way so that you can draw your bow or raise your gun. It sounds clumsy, but with just a little practice in the your living room, you will quickly get the hang of it. I use mine a lot, even when the temperatures are in the 20s and teens just because it is so comfortable. Anyone who has sat a stand all day, or even a half day, can tell you that even at those temperatures the cold eventually will settle in and make your stay uncomfortable. Check it out at www. Heaterbodysuit.com or by phoning (920) 565-3273.

tree when every sane individual is at home throwing another log on the fire or cranking up the thermostat another degree. But being too tough can cost you big time.

One morning before light I strapped my climber stand to a popple tree (that's an aspen to some of you), and walked the stand 30 feet up the straight trunk of the tree. A light breeze was blowing out of the northwest. It was 27 degrees below zero. Only the memory of a huge buck that I had seen in the area the day before kept me up in that tree all day. It was the coldest, most miserable day I have ever spent in a tree stand.

When shooting hours were over I had seen one deer, a fork-horn buck. When I tried to tie my pull-up rope to my muzzleloader to lower it to the ground and could not make my fingers do a knot, I knew I was in trouble. I had been sitting for ten hours in temperatures that I found out later had never risen above fifteen below zero. The human body is not built for that kind of torture.

To "walk" a climbing stand down a tree requires a certain degree of dexterity. Mine had been sapped by the cold. I stood in the stand and did isometrics in an attempt to restore circulation and get my muscles working again, but I was too far gone. No matter how hard I tried, I could not get my muscles to obey my mind. It was full dark now and I knew that I had to get down out of

that tree. I would not survive the night. I tried to unhook my safety belt, but I could not. Finally I managed to dig my pruning shears out of my pack and used them to cut my safety belt. Then with all of the strength and coordination I could muster, I heaved up on the seat of the stand and jerked the platform loose with my feet at the same time.

The stand and this hunter dropped fifteen feet in a heartbeat before the platform snagged on the stub of a branch I had cut off during my ascent that morning. When I jerked the two sections loose again, my plan was to slam on the brakes just before making contact with the ground, but with my lack of coordination, I misjudged and in an instant I slammed feet first into the snow covered, frozen ground. It felt like I had compressed every disk in my spinal column, but I managed to half crawl and half fall out of the stand and stumble along on legs that did not seem to want to go where I wanted them to.

A pack of wolves cut loose not far away and although I've never been scared of wolves or any wild animal, I did wonder if they could somehow sense that a potential meal was in trouble. It was a long quarter mile or so back to my truck. Thank goodness I'm in the bad habit of leaving the keys in my ignition, because I don't know if I could have gotten them out of my pants pocket. There is such a thing as too tough.

Index

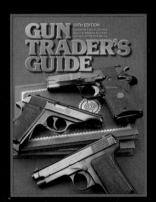
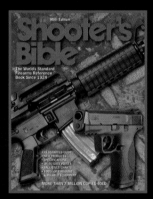

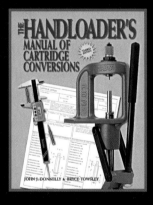